PARdon Me

PARdon Me

50 Years of Golf, One Hole at a Time

Joseph Bronson

SILICON
VALLEY
PRESS

SILICON
VALLEY
PRESS

Published by Silicon Valley Press
Carmel, California
www.siliconvalleypress.net

ISBNs: Hardcover 979-8-9858428-7-6 | Paperback 979-8-9858428-8-3 | eBook 979-8-9858428-9-0

Front cover art/photo courtesy of North Berwick Golf Club
Cover and book design by Mayfly book design

Library of Congress Catalog Number: 2024921180
First Printing: 2025

Contents

Foreword

There are famous professional golfers. But for many people, golf is a once-in-a-while thing, maybe three or four rounds a year. Other guys try to play a couple of times a month. Then, there are players who are out there every week, rain or shine.

And some, not many, who seem to live to play, will even make it to a Pro-Am. Joe Bronson is one of those guys.

Joe has managed a successful career in Silicon Valley tech while falling deeper in love with golf—for fifty years! Besides his raw talent, Joe has that honesty and honor that the great golfers have. The kind of curiosity you find in engineers and scientists, Joe brings to everything about playing golf: the balls, the equipment, but most of all, the courses and the holes, even the culture and the experiences.

From Pebble Beach to St. Andrews to Cape Kidnappers, Joe's details and specifics will put you right there. His descriptions of playing these courses—from course and hole design to the weather—are as vivid as the X's and O's of the 49ers playbook. You come away understanding what makes a course or hole a joyful challenge to play, or so awful that even the very best players can't make par.

Joe's ability to connect golf with the broader themes of our lives—ambition, challenge, adversity, and resilience—will have you assessing your own life experiences. It's a terrific read for any of us, from duffers to serious amateurs to professionals. This book will make you smile about the game we love, full of triumphs, calamities, and achievements that we can all relate to.

—Steve Young

Steve Young is a former professional quarterback who played 15 seasons, most notably with the San Francisco 49ers. Following a very successful career, he was inducted into the Pro Football Hall of Fame in Canton, Ohio, in 2005. His career in football and life has been marked by a consistent standard of excellence and drive for self-improvement. He founded the Forever Young Foundation in 1993, which is dedicated to the development and education of children. He is also an avid amateur golfer.

Preface

I have added this story as an opener to my book because, in a life filled with once-in-a-lifetime golf experiences, this one was more than simply unforgettable. The honor and great good fortune to play an iconic course with a sports legend ranks up there with GOAT memories for me. And it's memories like these that have motivated me to write each one of my books.

A Day with Arnold Palmer

It was another cloudy, gray spring day in Pebble Beach on May 4, 2002. I had driven down to our Pebble Beach home the night before to play in what I thought was a typical corporate golf outing at noon at the Pebble Beach Golf Links. I didn't know much about the event, other than that Arnold Palmer would be there, but the potential to play a hole with Arnold at Pebble Beach seemed like a great opportunity.

The invitation had come about two months prior, and I considered myself pretty lucky to have this opportunity as I was the only executive reporting to the CEO of Applied Materials who played golf. All the invitations from various tournaments and Pro-Ams that went to his office ended up in my inbox. I had played in a number of Pro-Ams on the Senior Tour, which I really liked because they were two-day events. The senior professionals had no problem playing with amateurs for two days. One year, I played in three Pro-Am events with Dale Douglas, who once asked me if I had a real job at the company.

May 4, 2002, was an unusual spring day at Pebble Beach. Pebble Beach has its own microclimate, where the area inside 17 Mile Drive could be consumed by gray cloud cover while Carmel-by-the-Sea, a mere two miles away, could be basking in brilliant sunshine. It was 11:15 a.m. as I entered the Pebble Beach Golf Shop just off the first tee of the course and announced my arrival for a 12:30 p.m. start time. The shop was quiet and devoid of any other players, which surprised me as I expected to see a bunch of corporate executives checking in for their assigned tee times. I assumed I would be placed in a foursome of corporate executives and get to play at least one hole with Arnold—who was there for a board meeting as one of the owners who had purchased Pebble Beach from its prior Japanese owners.

So when the golf pro behind the counter notified me that Mr. Palmer was waiting for me on the driving range, I was perplexed. The pro then proceeded to tell me that I would be playing the entire round with Mr. Palmer, Tom Siebel (the CEO of what was then Siebel Systems), and one of his executives. I was also informed we would be having dinner with Arnold on the property after the eighteen holes. Flabbergasted, I headed down to the range.

I never expected to play a complete round with Arnold Palmer or Tom Siebel for that matter. Tom is a Silicon Valley icon and remains engaged in the burgeoning field of Artificial Intelligence to this day. Applied Materials was a client of Siebel Systems, so I knew I would be warmly received. Still, I started to feel the "heebie-jeebies" creep in at the thought of playing golf with a true legend of the game.

Tom Siebel had hired a photographer to follow us around the course to memorialize the day. Unsettling visions started to cloud my head. Could I hold my game together? Would I be competitive? I hadn't signed up for this; was I good enough to be here? But soon, I started feeling more comfortable with the idea of being able to hold my own. I figured I had to be as good as Tom Siebel with my 6.5 index, and so what the heck—my only competition was myself, and I was going to have fun with it.

Arnold greeted me warmly and presented me with his famous umbrella pin, the logo of Arnold Palmer Enterprises. That umbrella pin has been stuck on my blue blazer ever since. Arnold was charming and affable, and for me, the ultimate surprise was there was only one foursome going to play on this day. I was blown away as there is almost always a cascade of fee players marching down the fairways at Pebble, and typically taking their sweet time doing it. It turned out that Pebble Beach management had closed the course, and we would be the only players to grace the links that day. I was about to play an entire round with Arnold Palmer—with Pebble Beach Golf Links all to ourselves! Sweet!

After warming up, we headed to the first tee, but the sky turned dark and gray with a bunch of ominous-looking clouds. The air was musty and humid, which is highly unusual for this time of year. As we got closer to the clubhouse, I thought I heard a clap of thunder and then saw a lightning bolt in the distance. Thunder and lightning are rare occurrences on the Monterey Peninsula. And thunder and lightning are the only things that will keep me off a golf course. I was immediately reminded of the last time this happened, in Osaka, Japan, the previous summer, where hot and humid conditions present myriad opportunities for a quick storm.

We certainly wouldn't be teeing off in this situation, as it started to rain a bit. It was eerily quiet and subdued, with little activity in the first tee area. It would be terrible if these conditions caused a washout, but I was convinced that it wasn't going to happen. We decided to wait it out at the adjoining Gallery restaurant for coffee and a snack. Arnold simply ignored the weather, as I'm sure he was also convinced that we were going to play eventually.

The Gallery is the Pebble Beach version of a diner, as it is strategically located by the first tee, where many players will fuel up before checking off their lifelong bucket list item—playing a round at the Pebble Beach Golf Links. As we entered the restaurant, we casually grabbed a table for four and ordered some coffee. Our conversations were short-lived, as it didn't take long before someone in the restaurant recognized that Arnold Palmer was "in the house," and we would be approached by one of the patrons, no doubt one of his countless fans. The whole place quickly recognized that Arnold Palmer was in their midst, and now the entire restaurant was coming over to our table seeking an autograph and a picture with him.

Arnold was unfazed by all of the fans and was amazingly gracious as he signed anything that was put in front of him. He took countless photographs with appreciative patrons. Arnold was enjoying himself as the activity was something he was used to, but he embraced these fans in a very humble way. It was classic Arnold—a true leader who couldn't have been nicer to these people. A little after 12:45 p.m., the skies cleared to blue, and some sunshine to boot, so it was time to amble down the stairs of the Gallery to the first tee.

The Gallery has a side exit—a stairwell that descends onto the grass behind the first tee. When we opened the exit door to go down the flight of stairs, we found the area completely packed with spectators. There were at least 500 people surrounding the first tee as the four of us moved to the gold tee. Word of mouth had spread that Arnold was here and was about to tee off at the Pebble Beach Golf Links. But . . . who were these other "turkeys" playing with Arnold?

The first tee now resembled the first at the AT&T Pro-Am. It was a thick crowd. As I walked up to the tee with my driver, the professional of Almaden Country Club in San Jose—where I was a member at that time—proceeded to ask me how in the world I was about to tee off with Arnold Palmer. I couldn't really answer the question and told him it was due to clean living and some good luck.

My expectations had now completely changed. On the driving range, I had convinced myself that I would be okay playing in this format, but I wasn't expecting to hit my first tee shot in front of an AT&T tournament crowd. Now it would be nerve-wracking hitting this tee ball—first, playing with Arnold Palmer and second, teeing off in front of this crowd which included my club professional.

Arnie tossed me a golf ball and told me to lead the way, which geometrically increased the pressure on me for this first shot. I gulped and grabbed the driver—the first tee shot at Pebble demands a straight shot of about 200 yards, whereas being right or left would eliminate the possibility of a shot at the green, and frankly, in these circumstances, would be truly embarrassing. While I was cognizant of the crowd, I had played in enough Pro-Ams to actually relish the pressure rather than succumb to it. I knocked the ball straight down the middle—225 yards and off we went. It was an exhilarating experience getting that ball in the middle of the fairway.

The weather on the front nine was sunny but very windy, even for Pebble Beach. We all played reasonably well, and my front nine 38 actually bested Arnie by one stroke. The difference was on the famous par 3, 7th hole of 107 yards. Normally, you're hitting a pitching wedge more or less downhill to this green surrounded by bunkers and the Pacific Ocean. On this day, we had a 40-mph wind directly in our face. Arnie commented that he had never played this hole with these types of wind conditions and spent some time deciding on club selection. He selected a four iron, and his tee shot veered off in a violent gust into the Pacific Ocean to the right of the hole. After seeing a shot like this from one of the best players of all time, my confidence hit rock bottom. I was undecided about club selection, and the reality of a 40-mph wind blowing in your face requires significant deliberation. I decided to follow Arnold with a four iron and had to make an effort to hit the ball hard and hope for the best.

The idea behind the four iron was to punch the ball from the elevated tee to cross the front bunker and pray that the force of the wind would keep the ball from flying through the green. I managed to pull this off as a gratuitous force of wind kept the ball on the green, where I two-putted for a par while Arnold made a double bogey. Arnie was nonplussed with his double bogey—champions realize that the game of golf is going to be an off/on experience, and his tee shot on 7 would be the last mistake he would make for the rest of the round.

Arnold told stories, made jokes, and generally made our day very special, which enabled me to be more relaxed and play better. My crowning achievement for this day was making par on the treacherous par 4, 8th hole. The 8th hole is one of the most difficult par 4s in golf, where the tee shot is no longer than 225 yards to the edge of a chasm that falls into the ocean below. The second shot is a carry of 180 yards to a treacherous multi-tiered green with a great drive to the chasm and a long iron to the green. If your tee sheet is not accurate, the shot over the chasm will be even longer with the ever-present wind conditions. Arnie played two wonderful shots on 8 and almost made birdie. He made it look easy while I was panting for good luck with my five iron. Arnie played very well on the back nine, shooting 37 to finish with a 76, besting my 78. Scoring really didn't matter though, as we all just enjoyed the day and the company. Arnold related stories, memories, and jokes that will last a lifetime. He also coached and was the ultimate raconteur on the golf course. And because Tom Siebel had hired that photographer, we now have the pictures to prove and memorialize the events of the day.

Arnold Palmer was the consummate gentleman and had an inner passion for the game of golf that I had never experienced, nor have I experienced since. There have been better players who have achieved more than Arnold on the golf course, such as Jack Nicklaus and Tiger Woods. Both Tiger and Jack may have more major victories, but no one has generated the excitement of a professional golfer since Arnold Palmer. Palmer possessed the skills of a champion but had a phenomenal inner passion for competitiveness combined with a professed love for the game. Beyond that, Arnie radiated a warmth, humility, and approachability rare among the top athletes in any sport. We could all relate to him. Arnold Palmer embodied, in the purest sense, the principles of the game of golf.

Palmer's achievements in the business and governance of the game of golf were unrivaled. The world of professional golf would not be in the shambles that it is today if Arnold Palmer were alive and well. He would have provided the leadership and business acumen that today's "guards" simply do not possess. Palmer had a lot to do with the success of the PGA Tour, and from his deep wisdom, he was always able to do the right thing. He became a major owner in the Pebble Beach Company that wrested the Links away from Japanese ownership that was ruining one of the game's iconic brands, and has ensured Pebble's legacy as a premiere commercial enterprise forever. His achievements in the game and the business of golf are unparalleled and unmatched.

It's been 12 years since that memorable day with Arnold, and I still cherish it as one of the greatest experiences I've had in playing this great game.

Introduction

I've been writing books on golf since the spirit moved me in the early 2010s. The idea was to write about golf from the perspective of the everyday player who is passionate about the game, but probably isn't going to be a Club Champion.

I also wanted to reach the non-golfer who believes that golf is a silly game, smacking a small ball around some green pasture. Golf is a microcosm of life, full of challenges, disappointments, and euphoria, all rolled into one experience. You can play miserably for 17 holes and then hit a 275-yard drive on the 18th hole and sink a 30-foot putt for birdie. You then forget the previous 17 holes and relish your return to the game for the next round.

Golf has an uncanny ability to sharpen your memory. My wife, Linda, can't believe how I can recall shots that I hit twenty years ago. I also find that golf, like life, progresses on a continuum, where it seems you never stop learning.

Today, I have reasonably good technique as I approach my late 70s. I could have had a better amateur career if, twenty to thirty years ago, I had the technique I have today. In those days, I got away with some poor mechanics despite my ability to score reasonably well.

I watch the perfection of the professional golf swing or the amateur college player and say to myself, "There's no reason I can't do that." However, my body—and specifically my back—then replies, "Sorry, you really can't do that."

It took me four years to write *Golf Chronicles*, my first book, self-published in 2016. My stories were scattered in files all over the place, and in my brain. I thought I would never finish that book, and, in my distress, I added an appendix on the dreaded "shank." I hate to even write that word.

It seemed like it took forever to get the book organized in a logical, readable fashion. After publication, I did some radio shows, book signings, and a lot of marketing to boost book sales. I also milked my business Rolodex and had companies buy copies for their external meeting events.

The motivation for the book sales was to generate funds, all of which are plowed back into donations or events for The First Tee and university golf programs. My wife Linda is not happy to see the number of college golf bags that populate the garages of our two homes.

The idea for the second book came quickly. This time, thanks to my blog posts, I didn't have to sort through a morass of half-written articles and notes. *Through the Green* was written in less than a year and seemed to flow seamlessly. I worked on it after Linda went to bed, usually around 8:30 p.m., and often kept going till 1 a.m.

I wrote parts of *Through the Green* in my backyard during San Francisco Giants games and West Coast Pac-12 games. The second half of the book came together mostly on coast-to-coast business flights from San Francisco to New York. I also decided to try my hand at fiction in book number two. The movie offers haven't quite rolled in yet, but I was personally satisfied with the work. *Through the Green* was also self-published, and both books won writing awards from various publishing reviews.

It turns out, writing a book is the easiest part of the project. Editing and production generate significant head trauma, lasting for months. The fun starts after the book is published, when you try to sell and distribute your work and get paid for your efforts. Fortunately, I had no illusions about commercial success.

Unlike my business career as an executive in technology, I had no contacts in the publishing field, so I delved into the world of bookselling on my own. I also experienced the world of rejection. I thought my books would be the perfect way for the business executive/golfer to pass the time traveling on a plane across states or internationally. I sent copies to Hudson, the largest airport bookstore in the United States, but they didn't even look at it. I'm sure my books went directly from envelope to trash, just like an unsolicited resume in a human resources outbox. I did a book signing at the local Barnes & Noble and the books sold out, but they didn't stock the book in the store. I did other book signings in local bookstores and sold out, but they never reordered either.

The biggest insult was the Pebble Beach Company, where I exhausted all of my contacts and became a qualified vendor. I imagined *Golf Chronicles* would be on sale in every book shop in the 17-Mile Drive, the Pebble Beach shop, the Spanish Bay shop, and gift shops everywhere. One day, I went into the Pebble Beach shop to look for the book on the shelf. I introduced myself to the staff as the author, and they were blown away—yes, my book sold out, but they never reordered.

I had similar experiences with *Through the Green*. But even though I started feeling like the Rodney Dangerfield of the golf writer's universe, I'm still having fun writing about golf. I started a website, josephbronson.com, where I write a weekly blog on golf topics in all areas of the game. To date, I'm approaching 300 blog posts, with a loyal following that keeps growing.

My followers asked me for a third book, and I spent quite a bit of time thinking about the format and content. And so, here we are with *PARdon Me*. It's another collection of unique stories from my experiences, along with my opinions on the game. Expect a complete menu of topics, from the PGA Pro-Am, pandemic experiences, and latest favorite golf courses (my new favorite being North Berwick in Scotland, which graces the cover of this book)—to updates from prior books on the best, worst, and hardest golf holes I've encountered lately.

And yes, be prepared for my update to the chapter on the dreaded "shank."

Personal Golf

For me, golf is fun, personally challenging, and an integral part of my life. It's my form of yoga, and it provides a sense of personal fulfillment.

I'm hanging on desperately to a single-digit handicap, which is edging toward double digits as my 70-year-old+ body refuses to conform with what my golf brain tells me to do. For the past four years, I've been taking lessons with an instructor who has been able to minimize this slide by reengineering my swing and tempo. I'm good enough to win competitively if I can maintain consistent swings under pressure.

I've played competitive golf and have won a few events, but as I get older, I don't feel I can compete against the younger generation. I'm fiercely trying to avoid having to move up to the regular tees or even the senior tees from the member and back tees.

So far, I've avoided moving forward, but it's getting tougher and tougher. At Pasatiempo Golf Club, I used to shoot in the high 70s and low 80s from the back tees; now I'm fortunate to pull that off from the regular tees. I've come to understand that it's all about club head speed, and I just can't generate the same speed I had when I was younger.

1. My Golf Traditions

Currently, my top priority is to play golf with my son. We've been playing together for thirty-eight years, and now he has a family and a 6-year-old son of his own. My son doesn't play often, but he has to play with me on Father's Day, my birthday, Black Friday, and one day during the Christmas holidays.

We've been to a number of NCAA Final Four events over the years (twenty in a row until the pandemic), and have always played two rounds at great courses near those events. In the New Orleans area, he made an eagle 3 at TPC Louisiana about 30 minutes before a thunderstorm hit the region and almost scuttled our round. We've played East Lake (Atlanta), Doral (Miami), Crooked Stick (Indianapolis), Houston Country Club (Houston), and several other great venues in the Final Four cities.

In Indianapolis, we played Crooked Stick on Easter Sunday, and I arrived without golf clubs. The course was closed for members during our afternoon tee time and no clubs were available to rent. With true Midwestern hospitality, the head professional gave me his personal set of clubs to use. It was a pretty nice gesture, and we really enjoyed the course.

My Black Friday (day after Thanksgiving) tradition is a direct statement against pent-up pressure on the presumed pre-Christmas holiday shopper and the relentless media advertising that promotes the joys of shopping. My response is to not go near a shopping mall or roadway on that day. Instead, I spend Black Friday playing golf.

The idea is to have the Thanksgiving Day meal at my home in San Jose, get a nap to induce digestion, then drive to our home in Pebble Beach for the upcoming Black Friday round. We are a family that has spent a grand total of $0 dollars and traveled a total of 0 miles on Black Friday for over thirty years. Imagine if this was a general trend: Black Friday would represent the beginning of an economic recession.

Another great day to play golf is New Year's Day. I consider New Year's Day another pathetic holiday with no significance whatsoever except that one day on the calendar has to be January 1. My motto is "avoid the holiday stress" and enjoy the pleasure and solitude of the game without the forced gaiety. You can usually get out and have a course to yourself by 1 p.m.

A newer tradition is playing on Super Bowl Sunday while the game is in progress. Many clubs host shotgun tournaments on that day, after which the participants proceed to watch the Super Bowl together—including football fans and those who haven't watched a game all year. These contrived joviality events are a big turnoff, and I proceed to the first tee with someone who generally knows little to nothing about football. There isn't a soul to be seen and we breeze through eighteen holes in less than 3 hours. Our timing is impeccable: we miss the boring half-time extravaganza completely, and get to watch the entire second half of the game in the club dining room without the Doritos and chili dips.

2. Playing Alone

Most people probably assume that golf is a social game, to be played by four players (foursomes) and accompanied by all sorts of gambling games to boost competitive spirit and camaraderie. While I would agree that group play is the primary format for the game, there's something about playing the game alone that offers a different perspective.

I don't think it's preferable to play golf by yourself, but I believe the experience has some of its own positive attributes. Golf is a cerebral activity intertwined with physical movement. It requires all parts of the body and mind to be in sync, controlled by brain functions like muscle control with the added psychological aspect of emotions such as confidence, frustration, anger, elation, and anticipation.

There's no standard when it comes to golf technique. Golf encompasses a complicated universe of swings that work and swings that don't work. People have proposed literally thousands, perhaps millions, of ideas and nuances for how to develop a golf swing. Millions of commercial products, gadgets, books, and articles by any number of pundits claim to possess the magic elixir of the golf swing.

Playing golf alone is an interesting experience. You miss the social aspects of the game, and some players look at you strangely—as if you're either a terrible player or a rogue personality that can't get anyone to play with you. When you play alone, the cadence of the game is different as you follow your own pace without being affected by the idiosyncrasies and habits of playing partners.

This cadence is important as you're trying to fine-tune a swing or attempting a few different shots, without overthinking any of it. There's also an ethereal aspect of the solitary playing experience, where you become more aware of the weather and circumstances around you. Conditions such as wind, fog, sunshine, heat, and even moderate rain create additional variants that you pay more attention to when you're playing alone.

The allure of the game of golf is that it really can't be mastered. No matter your level or handicap, the pursuit of improvement is the pursuit of the Holy Grail.

I've often wondered why the weakest parts of my game tend to shine when I play alone. It's a bit mind-boggling because you want to replicate this capability in your normal four-ball game or a competition, but it's elusive. The concept of muscle memory and the step-and-repeat function just doesn't connect for me. I suspect it's the basic skills of my swing and technique that continue to change as the years go by, with the constant hope for improvement.

I often compare my golf game to my basketball-playing days, where I never thought about my jump shot or free throw technique—I just expected everything to go in. It's the same at age 70 as it was at 16 (except for the height of my vertical jump). Why doesn't golf produce the same instinctual consistency as basketball? There's much more variation in golf, which requires much greater mental acuity accompanied by more mental variables than basketball. The result? It's easier to overthink.

After playing alone, I always find something to take away from the experience—perhaps a better shoulder turn, flatter swing plane, better putting stroke. To my dismay, the next time I go out to play with a group, none of these things tend to stick. It must be one of the many mysteries of the game.

Playing alone also has a downside: there are no witnesses to anything great or special that happens in your solitary round. A few years ago, there was a USGA ad where a young lad is walking, carrying his bag, and playing alone. He hits his tee shot, and the ball bounces once on the green and runs right into the cup for a hole-in-one. The kid grabs his bag and starts running toward the hole. The ball is in the hole, but he looks up and there's no one around. He knows that this wonderful shot, if unseen by anyone else, will not count as a hole-in-one. In the still of a setting sun, a guy nearby (unseen from the tee) on a farm tractor yells out, "Nice shot, kid."

Unfortunately, I once had the same experience but without the tractor guy. On the 8th hole at Almaden Country Club, I holed a 190-yard, 7-wood tee shot for a hole-in-one. The ball hit the middle of the No. 8 on the flagstick and simply dropped in. But it doesn't count—no witnesses. I looked around for anyone in the back yards of the adjoining homes on the hole, but no one was there. It simply doesn't count.

Another great aspect of solo play is the ability to focus on one shot at a time, and the objective of that shot, without concern about score. You can also experiment with clubs and yardages, which provides additional ideas of how to play certain shots. Professionals use these techniques to prepare for tournaments by playing solo and learning the course they are about to compete on.

Playing alone is a unique experience that allows you to simply concentrate on golf. It is actually therapeutic. It's my personal meditation practice, where I tune out the rest of my cares and worries and just hit a shot with the best stuff I have in the bag. I recommend it as an occasional exercise to reinforce how great the game really is at its basic level.

3. SLOWWWWWW Play

"That foursome ahead of us is still playing too slow. Fire a burst over their heads. Maybe that will get their attention."

Slow play is the curse of golf. Slow play has nothing to do with the game itself, but participants find various ways to perpetrate it.

For some unknown and irrelevant reasons, a golf game was meant to be played as eighteen holes in under 4 hours. I can find no source for this postulate. While many books and stories explain how the game became eighteen holes, none seem to specify why a round has this required timeframe. Who decided that eighteen holes should or must be played in 4 hours? It's not really a rule, but a guideline, and it differs all over the world. In Scotland, 4 hours is unacceptably long, whereas Japan has no standard duration, and a round there is considerably longer than 4 hours.

Many factors lead to or impact pace of play, so it's difficult to pinpoint exactly how to cure slow play. Pace is a state of mind, so each individual's approach can affect the tempo of the game. The player should consider pace of play as a key element of golf etiquette, which is a series of guidelines and in some cases hard rules. A good example is the lost ball rule, where a player has 5 minutes to find a ball, not 10 or 12 minutes, which can disrupt pace of play.

The first culprit in the slow play lane is the golf course itself and its management. Completing an eighteen-hole round in 4 hours translates to about 13 minutes a hole, on average. If you send a foursome off the first tee every 8 to 10 minutes, it won't be long before you have a clogged golf course, irrespective of how the players are playing. As soon as one group decides to look for a lost ball for 10 minutes, you instantly have a round where players are waiting on every shot.

The most annoying part of this is that the golf course is endorsing a standard pace of play, but really has no intention of following through on the rule. At Pebble Beach, all the practice balls have 4:30 printed on them to remind players that the standard pace of play for Pebble Beach is 4 hours and 30 minutes (photography included).

I would wager that less than 5 percent of the rounds at Pebble Beach are completed within that 4 hours and 30 minutes. After paying $600 to play a golf course, players feel entitled to get what they paid for. In this case, they'll play at a pace that suits them without regard for anyone else on the course. My guess is that the average round at Pebble is closer to 6 hours.

Pebble Beach is only one example of the slow play problem, as many other great venues have similar issues. Another horrible cause of slow play is disallowing the use of golf carts on the fairways. Too often, an unprepared player will choose the wrong club, then march back and forth to the cart, maybe multiple times, to get a different one.

This problem is directly the fault of the course, which should ensure that golf carts can enforce the 90-degree rule for approaching the player's shot. The 90-degree rule provides a path for reaching the ball while minimizing the area of the fairway that the golf cart has to traverse. At certain courses, the player actually spends more time going back and forth to the golf cart than they would to walk the course. This situation exists at all the Pebble Beach courses, and the best idea is to employ a caddy to drive the golf cart and do the running back and forth for you. Doing this saves a lot time and should be employed, but unfortunately, mandatory caddy programs are not in place on these courses.

Another slow play culprit is the PGA professional. You might wonder how players who hit golf shots so well can play slowly. The answer is usually found on the putting green, where the professional has to read a putt from every angle imaginable. The pros recently adopted an approach of stepping over the putting line to read the putt. All of these techniques are then adopted by the low-handicap, regular-fee, and high-handicap players alike, especially when there's some money on the line. At that point, the putting green begins to resemble a prayer service.

Amateur tournaments, and even scramble events, take over 5 hours per round, sometimes 6. Amateurs love to behave like professionals, but strutting around the green doesn't really reduce the number of 3 putts that will be recorded in the high-handicapper's round. Professionals could make a major dent in the slow play problem if they wanted to, but pace of play to the professional is almost irrelevant, as they are playing for their livelihood and feel that all these techniques are important to their competitiveness.

Slow play is a global problem, but one of the slowest places on the planet is Japan. The reasons for slow play in Japan are complicated and have little or nothing to do with entitlement. In Japan, a round of golf is treated as a social event. It regularly takes a few hours to actually get to the golf course, have some breakfast, get in some practice balls or warm-up, and head to the first tee. Then begins the first 3 hours of play.

At the turn, a mandatory full-course Japanese lunch, which takes an hour, is followed by a quick nap before the appointed back nine tee time. Three hours later, the round is mercifully over, and it's back to the clubhouse for fresh peas and beer. Nine to 12 hours have passed, and you are completely exhausted. You will sleep well tonight.

The complete opposite experience occurs in Scotland and most, but not all, of England, where slow play is not tolerated by the players themselves. The clubs don't really have to enforce any standards as a 4-hour round in Scotland is considered "slow."

Entitlement is a significant problem for slow play. The current societal norm is that rules are meant to be followed by someone else. You experience entitled behavior every day, such as people who think using their cell phones while driving is okay, even though it puts others at risk; the number of traffic deaths from distraction is well documented.

If you want to spend 10 minutes looking for a ball or a minute or two lining up a putt, then the groups behind you can wait. The concept of staying a hole ahead of the group behind is generally lost on most players. You've paid your green fees, and you'll play at whatever pace suits you without regard for the rest of the players on the course.

Just as some people won't stop driving with their cell phones in hand, the gods of golf are not going to solve the problem of slow play. The best solution, I believe, is for the golf course to enforce its slow play guidelines and respect the rights of all players.

For example, when I played in a tournament at Bandon Dunes, the course would assess a "slow play penalty stroke" if a round exceeded 4 hours—with no exceptions or excuses. All players were walking with caddies. Amazingly, with this rule in place for the competition, no penalty strokes were charged to anyone in the 72-person field. There are a number of private and public courses that enforce their slow play guidelines because the general membership believes in the guidelines, and those courses are monitored by assistant professionals, not retirees.

Slow play will continue to be a curse that golfers will want to avoid. It solely depends on each player's attitude and the willingness to do the right thing for all the players on the course.

4. Pro-Am Memories

Playing in the AT&T Pro-Am

The PGA Pro-Am is a wonderful event and experience for the golfer who can at least hold it together with a professional. The grand-daddy of them all is the AT&T Pro-Am, where the amateur gets to play three rounds of golf with a professional and has the potential to play on Sunday if the pro can survive the cut line.

The amateur must bring their A game and hope to compete alongside a professional who has a good chance of being high up the leaderboard. In these events, handicaps seem to resemble fiction. But at the AT&T, the amateur will have to play well for three days, and the difficulty and pressure of playing so consistently usually takes care of the raised eyebrows on handicaps.

One year, an overseas Japanese participant played to a handicap that was certified by the club professional at his home course in Japan. The Japanese player ended up winning the Pro-Am, but after some questions about his handicap, an audit revealed that the club professional was actually an employee of the winning player. His handicap was rather grossly overstated.

The participant was stripped of the title and his PGA professional teammate had to return the $25,000 he had been awarded. It was pretty embarrassing for the Japanese amateur, who was never invited back to the tournament. The entire episode was chronicled in an NCGA magazine article. Perhaps even Donald Trump wouldn't have done something like this but, of course, that's debatable. After all, Trump holds eighteen Club Championship trophies.

Most, if not all, of the other Pro-Am events on the PGA Tour are one-day events played on Wednesday before the pro tournament. On Monday night, there is a "pairing party" where the amateurs find out who they are playing with. Of course, all the big names, such as Tiger Woods, Rory McIlroy, and Jordan Spieth play with the title sponsors of the tournament, so it's not exactly an egalitarian process.

The tournament format is a best ball with a maximum score of double bogey to ensure that everybody gets around the course in 5 hours or less. Handicaps come into play, so your chances of winning this event with you playing your A game to your handicap are slim to none. Typically, it takes 20 under par or better to win a Pro-Am event, and the winning amateur looks like someone who could never break 100 on a par 3 course.

It's a wonderful experience if your professional is in a good mood. I've had the full range of experiences. I played in the Shell Houston Open with David Duval, and he didn't say a word to me for the entire eighteen holes—not "Hello," "How are ya," or "Goodbye." The Duval experience was truly an exception, though, as most PGA professionals are fun to play with. I played a few Pro-Am events with Loren Roberts, John Cook, and Curtis Strange and each of them was a great time.

My greatest experience at a Pro-Am was the 1998 Phoenix Open sponsored by Motorola, which occurred on Super Bowl Sunday. This was a once-in-a-lifetime event, as we would finish the Pro-Am and then proceed to the Super Bowl by helicopter.

At 7 a.m., I was on the driving range with Nick Faldo on my left and Tom Watson on my right, warming up in darkness for a projected 7:30 a.m. tee time. Every group had a PGA professional and an NFL football player. I played with Dan Pohl and Dan Marino. Lanny Wadkins was running up and down the line on the TPC driving range getting NFL players to sign footballs for him.

My wife, Linda, refused to come out to watch me. She was worried that I was going to pull a "Gerald Ford" and decimate the gallery with wayward shots. We proceeded to the first tee, and there were at least 1,000 people there to see Dan Marino. As Pohl and Marino hit their drives, my playing partner whacked a worm burner into the left rough on the first hole about 50 yards out.

I was a wreck, especially after seeing that shot, but I managed to compose myself and hit a driver 230 yards down the middle of the fairway. After that drive, the large gallery that followed us to see Marino no longer affected my game, as I just seemed to tune them out. On the 13th, I would hole a 50-foot putt for birdie and get a resounding high five from Marino, all in front of the ESPN cameras.

Despite that putt, my best Pro-Am highlight came at the Shell Houston Open Pro-Am in 1998, playing with Loren Roberts. In this event, three amateurs teamed with each professional. On the 14th hole, with water on the left side, my playing partners all smacked their drives into the water. My drive was the only ball on dry land, and my second shot to the par 5 landed at the bottom of a bush on the right side of the hole about 70 yards away. It turns out that the bush was uncooperative and would not move, and I faced an impossible shot. With my mates out of the hole, I decided to go for it and struck a 9 iron through the bush. I made great contact, and watched the ball head for the green, dead on line. It went in for an improbable birdie. The shot would make the ESPN highlights portion of Sports Center. Roberts laughed in complete disbelief.

I eventually burned out on Pro-Ams. It was fun being the only senior corporate executive in the company who played golf, so I captured all of the invitations. I played quite a few Senior Pro-Am events and at one point, Dale Douglass asked me if I really worked for a living, as I had played three events with him in one year. I won one of these events with Jim Colbert as my professional in Florida.

My Pro-Am career culminated in the opportunity to play in the AT&T in 2018. The invitation was really special since my son, Ian, was my caddy and my 2-year-old grandson, Adrian, would do some gallery time. I was paired with Roberto Díaz, a wonderful guy from Mexico who was struggling on the tour, but we had a great time and barely missed the cut. Roberto played well and made the professional cut, finishing 17th in the tournament. Nate Lashley was our professional partner in the group, who later found notable success after winning a PGA event in Detroit in 2018.

I started out strong with a par (net birdie) on the 10th at Pebble Beach and then birdied the par-3, 12th hole. I contributed pretty well that day, but we didn't have enough cushion as our third round was at Spyglass Hill following a huge rainstorm the preceding day. It's tough to make pars and birdies at Spyglass, and Roberto struggled with flu symptoms but played well enough to survive. Unfortunately, my game didn't wake up until the back nine, which was too late for us to make the Pro-Am cut.

Despite the beauty of the Monterey Peninsula, the top players in the game are choosing to skip the AT&T Pro-Am, which follows the Farmers Insurance Open in San Diego at both the North and South courses at Torrey Pines. The Farmers tournament follows the American Express Tournament at PGA West, which features another three-course event with amateur participation.

Increasingly, it seems that the professionals want to avoid the specter of playing three days with amateurs, which is negatively impacting the AT&T. The 2023 event drew only three out of the top 20 players on tour, with bouts of inclement weather throughout. The prestige of this tournament is under siege, and the organizers need to figure out a different format to attract the best players in the world.

In 2024, the PGA essentially "nuked" the AT&T Pro-Am by making the tournament a designated event, requiring all the top players to play in exchange for a greatly enriched purse. But the consequence of this change was that the Pro-Am's historical format essentially disappeared. The Clambake with its cast of entertainers and sports personalities was eliminated. Bing Crosby's legacy is no more.

5. Golf Is Hard

How so, you might ask? Let me count the ways.

Golf Is Hard
It's the first tee at Pine Valley.
Bunkers and junk everywhere,
intimidation and fear in the air.
How to navigate perhaps the toughest course in the land?
Where virtually every shot might end up in the sand.

Golf Is Hard
It's the first tee at Pebble Beach.
You can feel patrons at the Gallery Restaurant watching
 the trees on the right of the fairway look fetching.
 You've finally checked this one off your bucket list.
 The question is, will your swing persist?

Golf Is Hard
It's the 16th tee at Cypress Point.
The green sits 225 yards over the ocean,
But it looks even longer when your swing is in motion.
We know swinging harder doesn't make the shot right,
But emotion takes over, and messes your flight
The bailout to the left is a route we all know,
Yet it's bound to lead to a bogey or worse for this show.

Golf Is Hard
No matter the track, iconic or muni, for the professional, am-
    ateur, or daily-fee player
The first tee shot can be a real slayer.
The pressure is mental, no matter the venue.
Conjure your best technique and continue.

Golf Is Hard
Hooks, slices, pushes, and fades can make the round a sorry
    charade.
You don't want to participate in this type of parade
Tune out all the bad stuff—and focus on staying out of the rough.
The age-old question is: Are you tough enough?

Golf Is Hard
Out of the blue,
the dreaded shank can ensue.
There's no explanation for such an occurrence,
 As the club's hosel reacts to the disturbance.
Never utter the word . . . shank . . .
or you will never see the inside of a bank.

Golf Is Hard
On to the green to face the 4-foot putt.
The yips can occur for a permanent rut.
It's only 4 feet, but the green is so fast.
Your putt rolls 30 feet, in a horrible blast.

Golf Is Hard
Golf is the challenge to overcome all of these things
as we continue to seek the promise of sweet swings to retain.
These are the swings that bring us back to the game that continuously rattles our brain.

Golf Is Hard—Even for the Pros

Rory McIlroy is one of the best players in the world. In round one of the 2023 Memorial, he was steadily moving up the leader board playing with the leader, Jordan Spieth and Tyrrell Hatton.

McIlroy squandered some of his prodigious drives with indifferent wedge play and some not-so-great putts. He arrived at the 18th hole in second place and proceeded to hit a long drive that settled into one of the worst lies possible on the right side of the bunker.

His stance between club and ball was about 15 degrees, making any advance of the ball problematic. He managed to hit it about 20 yards and now had to focus on trying to make a bogey from 120 yards in heavy rough.

He knocked the ball out of the rough into another patch of spinach above the hole on eighteen. He then took another mighty cut out of that rough onto the green, where he two-putted for the magic snowman.

It was difficult to believe that a great round was destroyed with a bunch of errant shots occurring at the same time. This hole eventually cost McIlroy the tournament.

Yes, golf is hard.

The Ever-Changing Game of Golf

It might seem like golf is an "evergreen" sport. People who don't play the game believe it's somewhat ludicrous, hitting and chasing a ball for hours around a field to who knows what end. After all, every round has a few predictable aspects: clubs, balls, fairways, greens, rough, sand traps, and a water hazard or two. Golf traditions and rules go back as far as anyone can remember.

And yet, golf is constantly in flux, driven by both internal and external forces. We recently experienced a major external force—the COVID-19 pandemic—along with a couple of inside-the-sport issues that prove the malleability and resilience of the game.

6. The State of the Game (Pre-Pandemic)

In 2019, golf was in big trouble. The number of rounds played was decreasing, golf courses were being sold for housing developments, country club membership initiation fees were dropping significantly, and membership waiting lists disappeared. Golf took too long, was too hard of a game to learn and play, and was viewed as upper-class snobbery. Millennials couldn't be bothered with golf, preferring video games, workout regimes, cycling, and yoga.

I had been a member of Pasadera Golf Club in Monterey, California, a course designed and developed by Jack Nicklaus. Pasadera is a beautiful piece of property, and the course is a gem that also doubles as a private residential community.

The development is a few miles from the Laguna Seca raceway off California Highway 68. In 2019, the golf course was in pretty good shape, notwithstanding challenges with the availability and cost of water. Yet, despite all of its appeal, the private Pasadera club couldn't attract enough members to ensure its economic viability. The financial losses began to mount.

They were unable to sell enough houses on the property to break even, and club memberships were insufficient to sustain operations. Pasadera was sold to a Chinese investor then resold to a Chinese airline, but this did little to enhance the value of the property. The airline assumed it could attract Chinese émigré to join the club and Chinese tourists to visit, but their endeavors were unsuccessful.

In the 2010s, many nouveau riche Chinese people were purchasing housing in California for cash, with potential buyers scouring neighborhoods on bus tours to assess which private residences might be for sale. As the losses continued to pile up at Pasadera, an investor by the name of Donald J. Trump arrived on the scene with an offer to buy the club.

The short story of this experience is that the existing membership soundly rejected Trump's fire-sale terms and conditions, and the club reverted to ownership by a cross section of members and residents. Pasadera is only one of many examples across the country where golf course developments were at financial risk. Some of these projects were forced into sale, liquidation, or bankruptcy. Post pandemic, Pasadera has since been resold to a professional golf course operator and is flourishing.

Golf's popularity was steadily waning. The game was too hard to learn, took too much time to play, and was difficult to master. Municipalities all over the country started to consider closing the public courses they managed and using the land for residential housing to address the ever-increasing urban problem of home-lessness. And then, something happened to change this situation abruptly: the coronavirus pandemic.

Our lives changed forever with the discovery of the COVID-19 virus, which, by February 2020, was rapidly spreading throughout the world. Forced lockdowns isolated us all. We found ourselves without social gatherings of any kind. Golf courses, public and private, were closed as the virus raged through the country, along with uncertainty about how to avoid infection.

In California, the 17-Mile Drive, home to Pebble Beach Golf Course and a number of other courses, was closed to the public, leaving residents to enjoy the seacoast minus the traffic. In the absence of visitors, I was able to experience the iconic Lone Cypress tree, a Monterey landmark, for the first time after living there for twenty-seven years. Prior to the pandemic, the traffic flow of visitors to the Lone Cypress made it impossible to get close enough to see it. As the pandemic raged into lockdown status, I started hitting practice golf balls at my home in Pebble Beach, which borders the 13th fairway at Spyglass Hill.

We had been accustomed to a steady stream of players passing our residence on the 13th hole, but during the early days of the pandemic there was no one in sight. In April of 2020, somebody finally figured out that it was safe to be outdoors, and courses gradually began to reopen. But no one realized that the ability to get out on a golf course during the pandemic would trigger a renaissance of the game of golf.

Anything to get out of the house and actually do something was a step above playing video games, drinking too many cocktails, and watching too many game shows. Millennials started to look at golf differently, too. Golf became popular because it was something you could do with very low risk of coronavirus infection.

This situation was not lost on golf course management, who set up rules for playing golf in the open air. They established a number of safety procedures, especially COVID protocol rules regarding social distancing. And so, the courses began to gradually open up again.

Demand was significant, and tee sheets began to fill up in both public and private courses. Golfers literally came out of the woodwork to play. People who had never played the game before picked it up. People who previously complained about how long it took to play a round of golf stopped caring about the time.

Golf courses, especially marginal municipal golf courses on the brink of bankruptcy or at risk of being plowed under, became profitable enterprises. All these people needed golf balls, golf equipment, and golf lessons. The entire golf industry went from being a horrible business venture to a growth industry.

Some private clubs in danger of going bankrupt experienced a rebirth, with membership entry fees recovering to pre-pandemic levels. Other private clubs experienced significant new interest, raising membership entry fees and seeing the pre-pandemic "waiting list" phenomenon reappear.

Tee times at public venues began requiring significant planning, as rounds had to be scheduled two to three weeks in advance. In Monterey County, golfers had to wait three months or more for tee times at the Pebble Beach, Spyglass Hill, and Spanish Bay courses.

Still today, in 2024, demand remains strong. The green fee at Pebble Beach is $675, and there are four players teeing off every 10 minutes, 365 days a year. The recently renovated par-3 Peter Hay Golf Course at Pebble Beach has continuous play from sunup to sundown, with 5-year-olds to grandmothers participating. The interest in golf has achieved permanency among millennials' recreational activities. The new converts to golf have come to realize that golf is much more than hitting a ball around on some green grass.

7. The Golf Boom—Too Much of a Good Thing?

The golf business may be one of the few beneficiaries of the coronavirus pandemic.

By March 2020, most parts of the world were in lockdown, including golf courses. By April, somebody figured out that it was pretty safe to be outside and by May, golf courses were beginning to reopen. It's somewhat humorous thinking about it now, as pins had to stay in on the greens, and many courses installed devices that enabled you to remove the ball without touching the hole. Rakes were removed from the bunkers, as the prevailing attitude in those early days was that COVID-19 could be transmitted via surfaces touched by other humans.

During this time, golf was one of the few group activities that you could do outdoors. Private clubs started to reopen, though many didn't allow any guest play whatsoever. With the general restrictions on travel, especially by air, local golf courses became a primary entertainment venue, even for millennials. After all, how many video games can you play every day without going stir-crazy?

But by November 2021, the sport's popularity made it almost impossible to plan a golf outing anywhere. Even today, it's still difficult to book a tee time at many popular courses. Some examples:

- Bandon Dunes was completely sold out through 2022 and began accepting reservations for 2023 at the end of 2021! Today, Bandon Dunes is sold out through 2025. Oh, by the way, at Bandon, you pay up-front for your reservation, and you won't get a refund if you have to cancel. In 2019, I had to negotiate with the top of the company to get a refund for a player who was being treated for cancer. We actually had to supply proof to get the refund.

- Want to play Pebble Beach? In 2019, Pebble Beach was offering discounts and special deals to play the course. Now, it will cost you $675 a round, not including $55 for a cart. To play on this hallowed ground of American golf, you not only have to pay this outrageous green fee, but you also have to stay at the Pebble Beach Lodge for a minimum of two or three days in rooms that range from $800 to $1,500 per night. Foursomes go off the first tee every 10 minutes of every day of the year.

- Want to play the South Course at Torrey Pines in San Diego, home of the 2008 and 2021 U.S. Opens? If you're not a resident of San Diego, you can get a tee time by staying at the Torrey Pines Lodge adjoining the golf course. Ah, but 85 percent of the tee times are taken by San Diego residents, leaving the remaining times for people who stay at the Lodge. But what usually happens? The Lodge has rooms but there are no tee times, or there are tee times but no rooms.

- Want to play a public round of golf in Northern California? Be prepared to start calling well ahead of time. A collegiate golf team wanted to play a practice round before their scheduled tournament in Northern California. Three weeks before the day they wanted to play, I told them about many possible venues. Result: zero reservations available at any public golf course in the Monterey area.

All of a sudden, golf is cool. Price is no object. Public and private golf clubs alike are raising green fees to outrageous sums, and everyone is paying these fees. One private club charges a very high green fee, a cart fee, and a reservation fee (sounds like Spirit Airlines).

You can't even play in golf tournaments unless you book your spot well in advance. I was 65th on the waiting list for a club's member-guest event, four months before the event was held. For a tournament that I've been playing for years, held at the end of December, signups started in late August, and by September, there were no spots left. At national charity auctions, people are willing to spend thousands of dollars for a chance to play at some of the country's treasured courses in Long Island, New York, Massachusetts, and Florida.

Related sales of golf equipment, devices, and self-help tools are setting records. Golf club manufacturers frequently hold demonstrations of their wares, custom fitting their clients to tempt them into buying new equipment. In 2019, these manufacturers might have visited a club once or twice a year; by 2021, they were showing up every month. Golf teachers, who once seemed the province of the elite country club, are now in demand everywhere, and it's challenging even to schedule a lesson with a teacher. I need to book my teacher at least a week in advance and sometimes more.

All these factors have arisen due to the pandemic. Golf's renaissance is certainly not a bad thing, and it's nice to see the game taking a more prominent place in the world of sport.

The LPGA Tour is also as popular as ever, with stars such as Nelly Korda, who is now the No. 1 player in the world.

It's all good, but it's frustrating to those of us who used to have easy accessibility to the game. The pandemic-prompted participants are realizing what those who have played for years always knew: Golf is really a pretty good game. Even better than Grand Theft Auto!

8. California Bay Area Golf Thrived in the Pandemic

As the pandemic roared on through the country, it was encouraging to see the economics of golf prospering as it became one of the few activities you could partake in safely. Players who abandoned the game in the past because it was too difficult now appreciate the mental and physical challenges that golf offers.

One of the underrecognized impacts of the pandemic was the mental toll it took on all of us. During this time, golf provided a mental challenge that helped relax players and provide some reprieve from the daily grind of masks and physical restrictions. Golf might be another way to achieve the mindfulness and calm promised by yoga.

However, the mental side of golf affects players differently at different levels. At the highest levels, golf professionals tend to experience the most negative aspects of the game's mental side.

Competing professionally is difficult. The top golfers face mental challenges similar to those of top executives: decision-making, risk assessment (on the course), and financial pressures (off the course).

The professionals are all so good and so evenly matched that the difference between winning and losing frequently plays out on the putting green. Golf professionals seldom miss a shot, but they will also tell you that they only hit one or two excellent shots in a round. They have mastered the physical game, making the mental game paramount. They must integrate their physical skills into the cerebral exercise of hitting the right shot in the right circumstances, assessing and taking risks, and all the mental facets of putting.

At the highest levels, including the highest amateur levels, mastery of the "inner" game of golf is what separates champions from those who can't compete for a living and instead must settle for something less than the professional tour.

During the pandemic, golf helped ease the feeling we all had of being cooped up inside our homes and apartments without an opportunity to enjoy fresh air. The game is hard to learn but rewards players of all levels with some sense of achievement. I always find my golf game improves if I adopt a "glass-half-full" attitude, staying positive and knowing that better things might come—even if I just whacked it into the woods and lost my fourth ball of the round. My advice: Remember the good shots and erase the bad shots from the memory bank.

To play golf with any skill, you must stay on an even keel. Unlike sports such as football or basketball, there's no advantage to be gained through anger, aggressive behavior, or various oral expressions. Recalling the great shots hit during a round, however few there may be, brings you back to the game. How many times has a miserable round of golf ended with a 280-yard drive down the middle or a 15-foot putt holed for a birdie?

The game can be seductive, which so many new players discovered during the pandemic. Want a great example of the newfound popularity? Look at public play in the City of San Jose, California.

San Jose has three municipal golf courses: San Jose Municipal ("Muni"), Los Lagos, and Rancho del Pueblo ("Rancho"). In 2023, these courses saw a 65 percent increase in the number of rounds played. Before the pandemic, Los Lagos and Rancho were being eyed as potential targets for extinction, especially in view of the city's horrific housing deficiencies. San Jose Muni has been a mainstay for public golf since 1968, but the other two courses were fair game for destruction. Prior to the pandemic, these courses were bleeding money year after year as golf's overall popularity declined nearly everywhere. Because the pandemic changed the economics of golf courses, all three of these municipal operations are now operating solidly in the black.

During the pandemic and through 2023, San Jose's mayor, Sam Liccardo—who I believe is an avid cyclist and not a golfer—was not convinced that golf's popularity would continue to trend upward, believing that further commitments to public golf should be carefully considered. Liccardo's successor, Matt Mahan, has expressed doubts about continued taxpayer support for the city's municipal courses.

I submit that commitments to these three courses will provide long-term benefits to the community, financially and socially. As the pandemic evolves into an endemic, at least some of golf's new participants are more likely to stick with the sport than renew their addictions to video games.

The city wanted to divest from Rancho in 2010, and even then, local citizens protested and prevented the city from following through on its plan. Politicians proposed alternative recreational uses for Rancho, including turning the golf course into fields for other sports like soccer or baseball. Politicians continued to discuss and discuss until the capital costs of converting Rancho into alternative uses resulted in upside-down economics; the upfront capital costs could not be recouped by revenue.

Golf green fees produce revenue, so an increase in demand would make Rancho self-funding, able to cover its own costs of maintenance and supervision. Irrespective of the politicians, the future of Rancho is bright. Residents can participate in golf, and new players are coming to the course all the time. Other public and semi-private clubs in the area are raising green fees to levels beyond most patrons' means, leaving the municipal courses as the only affordable alternative for many players. In addition, Rancho provides access to The First Tee of San Jose, an organization serving local youth who would never have access to golf without their programs.

While the pandemic was a scourge for our communities and our country in so many ways, golf for the community of San Jose is now more affordable and accessible. It also provides more opportunities for seniors and youths through activities such as The First Tee.

As one local citizen said: "This is what you would really call a community golf course. I see every type of person here—older folks, kids, different nationalities, women. It's a big, big plus for us to be able to play right here."

9. Golf Balls

There's a lot of controversy about today's golf ball.

Professional golf pundits have been talking about the golf ball for the past few years, as players are driving the ball farther and farther. Modern players regularly hit tee shots over 300 yards.

In response, courses were lengthened to challenge the players. Augusta National is the most prominent example, while gems such as Pennsylvania's Merion Golf Club are considered too short to host major pro events. Some courses are as long as 7,700 yards, but the professionals are unfazed. Pros like Rory McIlroy and Jon Rahm regularly smash their drives 350 yards. Competing on the PGA Tour, or any other professional tour, now requires being able to hit the driver 300 yards. Considerable debate brewed for a while about changing the ball to reduce its distance and spin rates.

Then, the United States Golf Association (USGA) and the Royal & Ancient Golf Association (R&A)—the organizations governing the Rules of Golf—made it official. They adopted a new standard for the golf ball, to be applied first to "elite" competitors starting in 2028, followed by "recreational" golfers beginning in 2030. They were originally going to have two sets of standards, one for the elites and one for the rest of us, but sanity prevailed, and they opted for a unified set of ball standards.

The current ball has given the longest hitters on the PGA Tour a distinct advantage, but this rule change won't affect that advantage much. The longest hitters will see a reduction of 13 to 15 yards in driving distance. Average professional and elite male players will likely drive 9 to 11 yards fewer, with LPGA and LET players experiencing a 5- to 7-yard reduction.

The new ball standards will also resurrect the use of long-lost clubs like the middle irons. With today's professionals hitting 9 irons 150 yards, the game has seen the invention of the 450+-yard par 4 and the 600+-yard par 5.

I predict the USGA/R&A ruling will have very little impact on competitiveness in the PGA Tour. Players who are long drivers will continue to have an advantage over their lighter-hitting competitors. Tournament scores might drop a bit, but fans really don't care about the scores; they care about the level of competition. The only advantage I see in the revisionist ball scheme is that existing golf courses and some of the older gems will be more relevant and not have to be lengthened. There was some talk about an 8,000-yard layout, but the new rules should kill this idea.

Here's a short history of modern golf balls. Many years ago, there were two types of balls: surlyn-covered and balata-covered. Professionals generally hit balata balls, as they would travel farther and were easier to control. High handicappers typically wouldn't hit balata balls unless they wanted to spend a lot of money on golf balls, as they were easier to cut. Surlyn balls were the best option for the handicapped amateur; they were indestructible but harder to control.

Today, the surlyn and balata ball distinctions have gone the way of the dinosaur egg. Now the choices are between two-piece and multi-layer balls. There are a bunch of good brands, with Titleist leading the way. To take advantage of today's ball technology, you have to have swing speed, which at age 74 eludes me. So, I now have a different objective.

My new goal is simple: don't lose any balls. It's not a matter of money lost by having to buy golf balls, but rather a testament to my skill at keeping the ball in play. It's been an interesting run.

In 2021, I played seventeen rounds of golf with the same ball, only to knock it into the pond at the 18th hole at Los Altos Country Club. In 2022, I played nine rounds of golf in Scotland at Carnoustie, North Berwick, Royal Dornoch, Inverness, and a few others. With nine holes to go at North Berwick, I turned to my caddie and told him that this beat-up "Nike" ball had been in play for the last eight rounds, and we couldn't lose it. On the 14th hole, I promptly knocked my tee shot into the deep left rough, but my caddy miraculously found it. After holing out at the easy par-4, 18th hole, I had my playing partners sign the ball, and it now sits in one of the numerous ball cases I have in my homes.

I've since started another streak with a brand-new Calloway that continues to survive. I've now played six rounds with the same ball in England, Germany, and last week in Los Angeles. The balls aren't going far but they are going straight.

10. LIV Golf

NOTE: *The LIV golf situation is in constant flux. This chapter reflects my thoughts as of mid-2024.*

The LIV Golf Tour and the PGA Tour have brought the divisive nature of our society into the venerable game of golf. The LIV Tour remains a hot—and often polarizing—topic for the world of professional golf, as it continues to draw players from the PGA Tour, many would say underhandedly. The resulting discussions resemble the latest trends in USA national political discourse.

The tours could have coexisted amicably by taking players whose best years are behind them and providing them with a comfortable format and lifestyle that could have broadened interest in the game. The different formats that LIV is presenting with team golf could have been developed in a way to stoke fan interest. Instead of mutual cooperation and communication, however, LIV declared "war" on the PGA Tour, using the power of money to lure as many top PGA players into LIV by essentially buying them.

The money is generated from the coffers of the Saudi Arabian government's investment arm, funded essentially by the purchase of carbon-based energy products consumed worldwide. The Saudi government has a checkered history of bad acting, conferring few to no rights for women and taking unpopular stances on a host of other political issues impacting their neighbors throughout the

Middle East and Central Asia. Add the Genghis Khan of golf professionals in the likeness of Greg Norman, and you have the ingredients of a full-blown conflict.

Starting in 2022, a torrent of vitriol emerged from both sides, making professional golf look like a soap opera. It's unclear to me what Saudi Arabia is trying to accomplish, as LIV merely trumpets the reputation that they already have. I don't believe any amount of professional golf domination is going to change that image.

I believe the defecting players are clearly in it for the money and have decided to risk their eligibility to return to the PGA Tour if they don't like "exhibition golf." Which has proven to be a major issue. The PGA Tour does not allow LIV players to participate in any tournament or score qualifying points to determine their World Ranking. The four majors are inviting LIV players who are past champions of major events and have discreetly invited some based on their past performance. A proposed merger of the two tours was announced in 2023 but has not been consummated. Both tours continue to operate independently as the merger agreement has not been executed and expectations are all over the place. Professional golf as an entertainment venue has taken a major hit as rumors and speculation fly around constantly, and LIV continues to try to poach PGA Tour players. Professional golf is now beginning to resemble the soap opera-style conflicts of all the other major sports.

LIV is essentially the Harlem Globetrotters of professional golf, as there are no FedEx championship points or qualifications to compete in major championships in the U.S. or Europe. The European PGA Tour (DP World Tour) will not allow LIV players to qualify for the European Ryder Cup team. No one understands the team concept that LIV is trying to promote. Their TV coverage is on the same network that airs "The Real Housewives of Beverly Hills," and the coverage is impossible to understand as the leaderboards resemble the instrumentation panel of a Boeing airplane.

On the plus side, LIV opens opportunities for more young players from the Korn Ferry Tour to move up to the PGA Tour. The margin in professional golf is very thin. The players on the Korn Ferry Tour are all tour-caliber players who simply haven't been able to break through. Opportunities for those players will improve if LIV continues to poach players from the PGA Tour. LIV will also compel the PGA to improve the financial opportunities of its players through larger purses, and by making it easier for young players to realize their dreams of competing on the PGA Tour.

The success of the LIV Tour will depend on whether the PGA loses commercial sponsors, which would have a negative impact on some of the lesser-known events around the country. The PGA Tour has had a successful business model of attracting major commercial sponsors to support their events and contribute significant funding to local charities throughout the country in locations where the tournaments are held.

On the other hand, there's no doubt that LIV threatens the PGA Tour. The Tour will have to respond with changes, but they can't match the limitless coffers of the Saudi treasury. As a result, I believe that the future of LIV will be tied to two significant factors.

The first and most dominant factor will be whether LIV can secure major television rights to broadcast their events on national television. To date, LIV is generally ignored on major sports networks, and coverage is limited to streaming services. People need a degree of technical savvy, as well as the right subscriptions, to watch the events.

The second major factor, still to be determined, is whether the merger agreement between LIV and the PGA Tour can be executed. There has been no significant progress on this to date.

Media Potential of LIV

Television rights from the major networks are also a key element to tour success, and the Golf Channel presents significant coverage of these events. There was a rumor that the Saudis were interested in purchasing the Golf Channel as a vehicle to break the PGA Tour's stranglehold on the average golf fan. I think a sale of the Golf Channel (owned by NBC Universal) would be a blow to the PGA Tour. The question is whether the almighty dollar will overthrow the commercial sponsors of the PGA Tour, reduce PGA's televised audience, and impact the viability of various PGA events across the USA and Europe.

To date, LIV Golf has been unable to secure a significant TV partner, such as Fox Sports. Apple TV has spurned LIV Golf as "toxic." Politics aside, it seems that Fox embraces what might be viewed as divisiveness in one quarter and opportunity in another.

Fox's ascension as a national media brand really took off when it secured the rights to televise the National Football League as an alternative to the big three (ABC/ESPN, CBS, NBC) and became very successful and competent as a national broadcaster. The NFL is the most popular spectator sport in the United States; professional golf trails far behind.

Fox tried to break into the world of professional golf years ago when it cut a deal with the USGA to broadcast all of its major championships. I found watching professional golf on Fox painful to the point of having to mute the untrained musings of Greg Norman, coupled with a confused Paul Azinger and Brad Faxon. NBC and CBS have been successful in their coverage. Fox finally threw in the towel a few years ago as their approach to covering golf showed a significant lack of understanding of the sport. This was not the NFL.

Fox's attempt at covering professional golf can be best described as horrific. Joe Buck, for all his popularity in football, simply could not convert his skills to golf, which he has acknowledged. Having scantily clad Holly Sonders wax insipidly at the players, who spent their time ogling her instead of being interviewed, didn't add anything to the broadcast other than highlight how Fox presents things.

If Fox doesn't learn from its pathetic presentation of USGA, which bordered on embarrassment, the ratings won't be sufficient to challenge the play-by-play coverage of Jim Nantz (CBS) or Dan Hicks (NBC). LIV also lured away the entertaining rumblings of David Feherty, who could be a positive wildcard as a Fox broadcaster.

LIV could be successful with a softer approach that emphasizes the sport and accentuates the team format they follow.

Today, it's hard to tell what any of it means. There's so much money involved that it feels more like a celebrity quiz show, where the audience barely follows what's going on. Team Golf as a concept is not well understood. Golf fans, for the most part, don't even comprehend or support the PGA Tour Championship handicap system and qualification methodology.

It is interesting, but not surprising, that the Saudis are disinterested in the LPGA Tour, which has struggled for years to achieve financial prosperity. LIV could buy the LPGA Tour in a heartbeat, probably for a fraction of what it's paying some PGA players to defect. It's highly unlikely that LIV would make such a gesture, though, given that women in Saudi Arabia have limited rights. Some may go so far as to argue that women are viewed as necessary evils in the kingdom. The LPGA has a good product. The women's game is something male amateur golfers can better relate to than the 190-mph swing speeds of their male counterparts. The LPGA Tour is making great progress as the U.S. and Europe reignite global competitiveness with U.S. phenom Nelly Korda as the current World No. 1.

LIV faces the risk of losing out on the development of the players it poaches from the PGA Tour, while also not gaining recognition for its own talent. Today the PGA Tour is developing the players that the LIV Tour is trying to procure. The PGA Tour is likely to develop additional young players from the Korn Ferry Tour and USGA collegiate infrastructure who might dim the lights of the top players that the LIV Tour has plucked from the PGA Tour roster, which I believe is already happening. Of course, I suspect that LIV will continue to try to purchase the players that the PGA Tour has developed through the Korn Ferry Tour.

LIV could also benefit by copying the PGA Tour practice of making major contributions to charities in the venues where they play. Courting venues, such as Trump properties all over the U.S., won't be enough for the communities where these events are held to embrace LIV. Having protesters show up at your golf events doesn't help attract loyalty and sponsorship for the tour but seems only to add to the political divisiveness of the U.S. at large.

All things considered, the LIV Tour is not going to go away, and while all of this banter is interesting, it's becoming very boring. There are positive and negative points on both sides of the argument but, in the end, the almighty dollar will prevail. Golf fans will decide based on what they watch, stream, or support. There's also no question that the players will also decide, as they are independent contractors and free to do what they believe is best for them. It seems inevitable that both tours will have to figure out how to coexist, as the game of golf is far more important than all of this. Professional golf as an entertainment is being negatively impacted by this split and will continue to deteriorate until some agreement with the PGA Tour is achieved. If the Saudis try to buy the PGA Tour, it seems to me that the U.S. government anti-trust arm will take a dim view towards that type of purchase.

The good news is that golf is a sport for all of us to participate in, at whatever skill level we have. It will persevere. The professional golf world will always exist, irrespective of what happens to these competing tours and our views about them. But it's a shame that divisiveness has come to the world of golf in almost the same way as in our political spectrum.

My Local Golf Scene

I've had the great good fortune of playing rounds of golf all over the world, at courses famous and unknown. Still, it's a pleasure to come back home to Monterey County, California, with the wealth of wonderful courses within an easy drive. In my case, there's some truth to the old adage: There's no place like home.

11. The Twilight Round at Pebble Beach

I love playing Pebble Beach. Living a mile away from the first tee, I hear Pebble as a voice that ruffles through the trees of the Del Monte Forest and beckons me onto the track.

The rub with playing Pebble Beach is that every other golfer on the planet wants to play the course as well. It's probably on every golfer's bucket list. To accommodate the crowds, Pebble Beach sends a foursome off the first tee every 10 minutes, 7 days a week, 365 days a year—except during tournament play such as the AT&T Pro-Am in February and a senior event in September—at a price of almost $700 per player. I imagine they could raise the green fees to $1,000 without any impact on the number of players.

The problem with playing Pebble Beach is twofold. First, pace of play is generally poor. So many people are playing the course for the first time, and they lack knowledge of how to navigate it, especially putting on the greens. Second, players don't want to play quickly. They want to soak up the experience, so etiquette on pace of play is usually ignored. Pebble management has marshals patrolling the course, but they are loath to scold or encourage anyone to speed up. It's always curious to me why they are out there in the first place.

Another cause of slow play is that golf carts are permitted only on the cart path but are not allowed on the fairways, which makes no sense. This rule does nothing to enhance the player's experience. Watching the group in front of you traipse back and forth to a golf cart, not knowing what club to select on their bucket list course, will make for a long day for everyone.

I often thought about being the last player on the course as I drove by the 15th hole on 17-Mile Drive, seeing no one on the 15th hole or the 14th green. One glorious August summer day, when I hadn't played Pebble in a while, I decided to get the last tee time, 3:30 p.m.

I warmed up at Pebble's antiseptic driving range, which has very little character. I've always felt (rightly or wrongly) that Pebble exudes an aura of polite arrogance. They are on everybody's bucket list, and they know it. They come across as somewhat welcoming, but actually, they're not. The practice balls are all marked 4:15 p.m., intended to guide you to play your upcoming round in 4 hours and 15 minutes. In actuality, this is merely a paid political advertisement against slow play, without any substance.

Unlike Pebble, at Bandon Dunes, Oregon, you will find nary a hint of arrogance. They want you to play golf and play as much as your body can bear. Everything they do at Bandon is to facilitate your experience playing golf. You get the feeling they want you to have a good time.

At Pebble, the attitude is, thank you for your green fees, but we don't care too much about your experience because we know you were literally dying to get here. Enjoy it and begone. At Augusta

National, a guest is treated exactly like one of the members, and the place simply exudes class without arrogance.

My feeling is that Bandon and Augusta National want you to have a great day playing their great course. At Pebble, they want you to have a good time, but you will do what they say and enjoy it. They imply, "We endorse a 4-hour and 15-minute round, but we all know you will never comply with making it happen, and we really don't care if you make it or not."

After hitting a few balls with my partner at the driving range, we rolled up to the first tee for our starting time. Of course, there's a group going off at 3:20 p.m.. I'm already disappointed since I'd expected that no one would risk darkness by playing at that time. My plan to have a leisurely stroll through the course was already at risk, as darkness falls at 7:45 p.m. in late August. Already, the scheme was a complete failure.

I assessed the group in front of us and instantly knew they had no knowledge of the course. This was not going to be the smooth walk in the park that I had envisioned. To add further insult to injury, we were joined by two other players from Maryland, and that was the coup de grâce. They were very nice guys to play with and were able to keep up and play reasonably well, but alas, the group ahead of us paced themselves like a broken-down school bus.

We got to the 10th hole at 5:50 p.m., and I knew our daylight finish was in jeopardy. The course was in great shape and very playable, so there were no excuses. On the 11th hole—a par 4 where you turn inland from the sea—I impatiently informed the group in front of us, who were now on the 12th tee, that we had only an hour of daylight left. They looked at me as if I just arrived from Mars, and had no intention of speeding up.

Dusk set in on the 17th. After a good tee shot, I holed a well-struck putt with no visibility. The challenge was now to play the venerable 18th in complete darkness. I had the confidence and local knowledge that if I could keep the ball in the fairway, I'd be able to locate it and hit it again. Two shots in the middle of the fairway, and I couldn't see anything, so I hit a 5 iron into the front bunker. The good news here is the green has some illumination from its proximity to the lodge. I managed to get up and down from the bunker for a closing par in the dark. It was 8:20 p.m., and we'd been playing for 4 hours and 50 minutes.

So much for the marking on those practice golf balls. An experiment gone wrong and never to be repeated.

12. Pasatiempo Golf Club

Pasatiempo Golf Club is a relatively unknown gem throughout most of the country, but well known as a must-play for Northern California golf enthusiasts. The Santa Cruz County course is a famous Alister MacKenzie design and is probably the toughest 6,500 yards that a low handicapper could ever play. The holes are so strong throughout that the course could prove a very difficult test for anyone.

Pasatiempo was closed to outside (public) play in April 2023, following the Western Intercollegiate amateur championship. The course is semi-private, with a private club membership structure and public play that starts at 10 a.m. on weekends. The fees from the public side essentially provide the funds to operate the course; unlike private clubs, there are no annual dues.

As of this writing, the course is being renovated. All the greens will be replaced with bent grass, and the bunkers and short-game area will be upgraded. The course was open to members only at the time of closure, but after a short period, guests of members were allowed to play. The renovation is being completed nine holes at a time, so the entire course isn't impacted all at once.

Members are now playing the back nine twice for a full round, with two pin positions on the green. The first nine holes are played to one flag color, and the second nine holes are played to a flag of a different color.

When I played the course in this configuration, I was struck immediately by the quiet and the pace of play. Normally, the course is a beehive of activity. On weekends, after public play begins at 10 a.m., the course lacks the feel of a private Top 100 golf course. With the public on the course, there are plenty of unfilled divots in the fairways and on the greens, coupled with slow play. Given the difficulty of this course, the average pace of play probably exceeds 5 hours.

On one quiet Friday, the golf course spoke loudly. The fairways were manicured, free of the bad behavior of unfilled divots. The pace of play made you feel like you might be at Oakmont or even Pine Valley. It was quite enjoyable to witness the majesty of this great golf course design reassert itself. I was so impressed, I had to postulate that the club should perhaps reevaluate its status and become much more than a semi-private club.

So, my question now: semi-private or private?

After playing that idyllic round at Pasatiempo, I was convinced that it should transition to a private golf club. The course is so pristine when it's not under stress from public play. I believe a privatized Pasatiempo would launch it into the top 20 courses in the country.

I don't have any detailed financial figures, but I ran some estimates to assess whether a private-only model is feasible. Financially, members currently buy in at a cost of $200,000, with no annual fees. Unlike other private clubs, where members frequently pay annual fees of $15,000 to $20,000, Pasatiempo relies on revenue from public play to cover the expenses of running the club. Members are charged no assessments for improvements or required maintenance.

I would estimate that the public plays between 15,000 and 20,000 rounds per year. If this is close to being correct, this would amount to $6 million in green fees, and probably another $1 million in ancillary fees. If the public rounds were reduced to 10,000, public round revenue would be reduced to $3 million—but I would increase the green fees to $400, raising another $1 million in revenue.

If every member added $50,000 to their initial investment in the club, the club would raise $20 million. That amount is enough to cover almost seven years of lost public revenue, while significantly improving the condition of the golf course and its ambience. Raising the club entry fee to $250,000 would also cover future costs and potentially provide some enhancements such as rebuilding the "sad" driving range. Most public course driving ranges are better than the one at Pasatiempo.

While these changes might be unacceptable to current members, the notion of Pasatiempo as a top 20 golf course in the country is compelling. The course comes alive, as if MacKenzie himself is asking for something special.

13. Monterey Peninsula Country Club— Dunes Course, 14th Hole

The 14th hole on the Dunes Course at Monterey Peninsula Country Club is the course's signature hole. It's the only golf hole on the Monterey Peninsula that crosses through 17-Mile Drive. Tourists and locals alike get spectacular views of the ocean at all the lookouts on 17-Mile Drive. At the Point Joe lookout, where the 14th hole is located, they get an additional treat, forming a gallery to watch the players try to cross the boulders, bunkers, and fescue to get to the green.

It's interesting that the gallery watches in silence, which I find quite extraordinary compared to the fans that watch professional golf. The back tee is carved out of the rocks and measures 180 yards. Players trudge to the tee on a dirt path, past the rocks onto a small piece of turf that resembles a miniature helipad. The prevailing wind blows right to left over all of the boulders, fescue, and other hazards, and you're going to have to start your ball toward the ocean with the idea that the wind will blow it back onto the green.

Most of the gallery are tourists who don't believe that any of us will be able to hit our tee shot onto the green. There are two strategically placed bunkers, one guarding the green on the right and one on the left. The bunker on the right snares tee shots that just make it over all the boulders but don't carry the green. The bunker on the left is devilish, placed there to catch the shots carried by the prevailing wind. This bunker gets visits from many players.

Club selection on this hole is critical, as running a tee shot through the green will require a delicate chip shot back onto the green. I generally use a 7 wood in the normal 10 to 15 mph wind, move up to a 3 wood with the wind in my face, or a 7 iron if the wind is at my back (rare for this hole). I've also hit an 8 iron on occasion in downwind conditions. The green is large for a par 3, but the combinations of all these factors are intimidating for the medium to high handicapper. The low handicapper has to focus and pay attention to the wind and all these factors. Birdies on this hole are to be cherished.

In the California winter of 2023, the area was pummeled with a series of storms labeled "atmospheric rivers." These storms crunched the 17-Mile Drive infrastructure, yielding downed trees and power lines, and resulted in power outages throughout the Del Monte Forest. One of these storms was pretty severe. But in the pouring rain, a few brave souls were playing the hole when huge swells emerged from the sea, forcing the players to run away to higher ground as their golf carts were stuck in an instant mud bath.

The ferocity of the tides moved the boulders that shape the hole from tee to green, making it impossible to get to the green.

The bunkers and green took on a considerable amount of seawater, and it looked like the hole would be out of commission for a while. I received texts and notes from people all over the country who feared we had lost the entire golf course to this storm.

The good news was that the signature, lonely cypress tree behind the green survived an onslaught of 50 to 60 mph winds and is still intact, with the same leaning posture from right to left, which is the indicator of the prevailing wind. The MPCC staff performed a minor miracle getting the 14th hole back into service in three days. The key was removing the saltwater from the green and re-sodding some of the bunkers. Boulders that the sea tossed around during the storm were restored to their former position.

14. Cypress Point—16th Hole Ace

SMU freshman Christian Clark knocked a fairway wood over the Pacific onto the 16th green at Cypress Point Club and directly into the hole for an ace. There were plenty of witnesses to this shot, which has to be one of the most exhilarating golf shots that Clark has ever hit in his young life. The SMU golf team was playing a practice round prior to their appearance at the Cal Poly Invitational, which was being held at the Santa Lucia Preserve, known throughout Monterey County as simply the Preserve. Clark, who hails from Dallas, Texas, had never played Cypress before.

The 16th at Cypress is one of the most breathtaking holes on the planet. It's also one of the hardest and most intimidating holes to play. The only thing between the player on the tee and the front bunker guarding the green is the Pacific Ocean. The carry from tee to green is 230 yards without any wind (and there's always wind!). There's a bailout area about 175 yards on the left for those players who are content to turn this hole into a par 4. Collegiate golfers as a group tend to be fearless. Exemplifying this stereotype, Clark's shot was a well-struck fairway wood.

My best experience at the 16th occurred when I took a driver, flew the green on the left, and landed on the beach. The beach is not really a beach but a pile of sand and rocks sitting at least 50 feet below the green. You could hit a drive through the green, but it would land in a cluster of rocks and debris, probably resulting in a lost ball.

Up to this point I was having a pretty good day at Cypress, but I was bracing myself for the inevitable drop and probable double bogey. However, it was low tide, and my caddy proceeded down to the beach and spotted the ball sitting on the wet sand. I was prepared to take my punishment, but the caddy told me to come down to the beach to hit this ball. I looked at him as if he had just landed from Mars and told him it was an impossible shot. His reply: "You got this, just hit the ball and don't take any sand."

The ball was sitting up nicely on the wet sand, but there was a 50-foot rock wall between me and the green. My caddy went back up to the green, offering himself as the target. "Open the club face and just hit it over my head and don't worry about it."

I selected a pitching wedge. I was drained of feeling, almost numb. Hitting the ball from this position would be, at best, a "small miracle." I grabbed a pitching wedge and decided to go for it. The ball would have to be struck perfectly to get airborne to clear the wall and get on the green. My only idea was to hit the shot high enough to at least get over that wall.

With saltwater beginning to seep into my shoes, I grabbed my pitching wedge and hit the shot. The ball sailed over the caddy's head. I couldn't see the shot from the beach, but the caddy screamed and yelled, "Eight inches!" An improbable par would be recorded. I just shook my head and said, "You could give me another 100 balls and I would never again be able to pull off this shot."

The 16th at Cypress is probably the closest hole to hallowed ground in the world of golf. Playing it is truly a standout experience. Chris Clark will never forget his hole-in-one on what is one of the greatest holes on earth.

15. The Eagle Has Landed

This is the saga of an unusual shot by an unusual player. The protagonist in this story is Todd Tuomala, a member of Monterey Peninsula Country Club. One thing you should know is that Todd has a love/hate affair with his driver.

Playing the MPCC's Dunes Course, Todd had just made a remarkable par on the difficult par 5, 15th hole, following a less-than-serviceable tee shot into the left bunker. The 15th has a bunch of well-placed bunkers, but it also has one of the widest fairways on the course, so landing in the left fairway bunker is "not so good." After a great shot out of that bunker, he holed an 8-foot putt to make the par.

Then he stepped up to the 16th tee. The 16th is a dogleg to the left, with a bunker on the left all the way from tee to green. His driver failed again, as the ball faded into the massive left bunker lining the entire hole. This is a waste bunker, allowing the player to ground the club.

As the giant bunker meanders down to the green, additional standard greenside bunkers guard a green that measures at least 25 yards horizontally. The green is so large that it hosts two very different positions: extreme left and extreme right.

The extreme left position is very difficult as the green may be huge horizontally, but it is small vertically, probably less than 20 feet. A shot into the extreme left position has to be hit very high to carry the front bunker and land soft enough to avoid flying the green to a terrible position of sand, stone, and muck. Another factor is that the series of trees inside the left bunker completely blocks the player from having any shot at the left pin position.

On this day, the pin position was extreme right, which makes the hole receptive to a short-iron shot. For the extreme right pin position, the green slopes severely from right to left. Todd's tee shot was in a terrible position in the waste bunker. He's left-handed, which made the shot difficult to even extricate the ball from the bunker. The safe play might have been to get the ball to a 50-yard position, then try to get up and down from there.

Todd had no intention of chipping back and playing it safe to try to make par. He had a decent lie in the bunker but was blocked by a tree. Let's just say that this shot was a high degree of difficulty with a potentially very bad ending. The only shot possible was to aim right of the hole and hope to fade the ball toward the green. I'd rate this shot a 10 on a 1–10 scale, with 10 being the most difficult.

This is the shot that *Golf Magazine* tells you never to try—don't be a hero, take your medicine, lay up, and try to make par.

Todd was about 180 yards away and grabbed his 6 iron. I stood in the middle of the fairway to watch, feeling satisfied like the cat that ate the canary, my ball sitting 110 yards out with a perfect lie in the fairway. If this were match play, I would have counted on winning this hole easily.

Todd took the 6 iron back and made a mighty rip. The ball was smashed and headed to the right side of the green. To my amazement, it hit the green some 30 feet from the pin. I watched incredulously as the ball began to pick up speed and head for the hole. After at least 4 or 5 seconds, it was definitely going in—and it did! EAGLE 2!

Most eagles are holed from the fairway with an excellent iron shot. But Todd chose the most challenging route possible, and this shot was at the peak of the difficulty scale. A wager placed on Todd making eagle here would have bankrupted Draft Kings. Oh yeah, by the way, I hit an indifferent wedge to the green and made par.

Golf Holes

In this section, I document my personal experiences playing golf holes that have impressed me with their uniqueness. For the first time, I have selected the best and most difficult par 3s I have ever played. The par 3 presentation is followed by another version of the hardest and worst-designed holes I have ever encountered.

16. Par 3s

This chapter lists the best par 3s I've ever played, by hole. There are a number of outstanding candidates for "best." I'm ignoring any of the par 3s with artificial lakes and ponds that dot the courses on the PGA Tour.

Hole 1
Royal Lytham & St. Annes Golf Club
Lancashire, England
206 yards

Royal Lytham is the only Open Championship venue that opens with a par 3. The hole is 206 yards with seven bunkers. Bunkering is a trademark of Lytham, as the course has over 150 of them. The hole itself is pretty straightforward, but you have to avoid the bunkers to make par or better. The green is fairly large and reasonably flat. The hole will live in infamy from the Open Championship in 2001. Ian Woosnam was tied for the lead and playing in the last group. He teed off with a great shot and holed out for birdie when disaster struck. His caddie motioned to Woosnam, "Boss, we have a problem." He had two drivers in the bag for a total of fifteen clubs, one more than the maximum allowed. The two-shot penalty turned a birdie into a bogey, and Woosnam never recovered. He was very upset, but the responsibility for the golf bag lies with the player, not the caddy. Woosnam didn't fire his caddy that day but ended up firing him a few weeks later when he failed to show up for his tee time. Woosnam would finish 3rd in the Championship behind David Duval.

Hole 2
Bandon Dunes
Bandon, Oregon
155 yards

How can a par 3 of 155 yards, other than the 155-yard Golden Bell at Augusta National, count as one of the most difficult par 3s on this list? It shouldn't, but it does. Every time I've played this hole, it's been in the morning with an early tee time. The Bandon Dunes morning is routinely cold, high 30s or low 40s, with gray skies and clouds in abundance. Assuming no rain in the forecast, the sun might not come out and warm things up until late morning. You have just played the gentle par 4 doglegged first hole, hopefully well, because you will have to concentrate hard on No. 2. It's a reasonably long trek up the hill to No. 2, but the hole, in the morning gloom, has a bizarre air about it that can spell trouble. As you approach the tee box, the hole looks a lot longer than 155 yards.

It's uphill and it's cold, and the ball doesn't travel well in these conditions. When you look at the back tee of 189 yards, it looks like 230. Your performance on this hole will be highly correlated with your score on No. 1. Without wind and clouds, a good 5 iron should land you on the green and give you a decent opportunity for par. The green is large and full of undulations, so even when conditions are calm and sunny, birdies and pars on this hole are few and far between. However, missing this green will require a brilliant chip shot. In fact, because you can get all kinds of weird lies around the green, you're better off in the bunker. This par 3 is an illusion: looks easy on the card, looks doable on the tee, but . . . while this No. 2 doesn't present the historical drama of Golden Bell, it's a hole that can evoke significant surprise. And not in a good way.

Hole 3
Pasatiempo Golf Club
Santa Cruz, California
205 yards

The 3rd hole at Pasatiempo is an absolute beast, measuring 205 yards straight up the hill and surrounded by bunkers. The entire hole slopes from right to left, which you won't feel if you're playing the hole for the first time. A tee shot that comes up short on the left will either die in the thick heather or meander into the middle of the fairway. A tee shot that comes up short on the right will either land in the trees on the right or roll to the bottom of the hole, requiring a chip shot over the menacing bunkers that surround the green. Any miss of a chip shot on this hole will likely result in a double bogey or worse.

The bunkers surrounding the green require significant skill to get anywhere near a pin position. The tee shot has to carry the entire length of the hole, as any shot that lands short of the green can roll down the hill at least 30 to 50 yards. Chipping into this hole is also treacherous, given the significant right-to-left slope of the large green. In dry conditions, I've seen a tee shot that's a yard short of the green end up almost 100 yards down the hill. The green is very difficult to putt; all pin positions are devilish. It might be the most difficult par 3 hole on the planet. You can make some very big numbers on this hole due to its upward sloping combined with a very large green and a bevy of bunkers on all sides of the hill. It will give Pine Valley No. 10 some competition for one of the most evil par 3s in golf.

Hole 3
Mauna Kea Golf Course
Big Island, Hawaii
205 yards

The 3rd hole at Mauna Kea must be a contender for one of the greatest par 3 holes in the world. Unlike at Pasatiempo, the challenge is reasonably straightforward but daunting. The tee shot has to carry 185 yards from the back tees (170 yards from the regular men's tees) to get on the green. The carry is completely over the ocean, so you either make it or feed the fish and head for the penalty area. The hole combines difficulty with absolutely spectacular scenery. With the Pacific Ocean on the left, the carry is over the lava that forms the base for the hole. There's not much in the way of a bailout area, as you would have to have hit a shot at least 150 yards to the right, leaving a very difficult pitch onto the green. The green on this hole is immense. Three-putting is a definite risk to par, even if you're fortunate enough to make the green with the tee shot.

Hole 3
The Olympic Club, Lake Course
San Francisco, California
202 yards

This is a gorgeous hole with a large vertical green that is quite narrow for its length. The elevated tee has bunkering on both sides of the hole. The hole is a bit intimidating, as accuracy is required to carry onto the green. The air at Olympic is generally cool and moist, coming off the shores of nearby Lake Merced, and the climate conditions seemingly negate the downhill advantage. Also intimidating is the largely vertical shape of the hole, which doesn't leave much room to miss the bunkers on either side. The green's shape presents little real estate to work with, so getting up and down rates a high degree of difficulty. Cool, crisp air also makes club selection difficult because it can offset the impact of the downhill, thus making the hole play at its specified yardage.

Hole 4
Royal Birkdale Golf Club
Liverpool, England
199 yards

The 4th hole at Birkdale has only one thing to say as you approach the tee box: "You better have enough club." The most intriguing feature of the 4th is the length of the hole, which becomes obvious when you stare straight ahead to assess the wind and conditions. The hole looks pretty straightforward, having three bunkers on the left and one placed strategically on the right. The placement of bunkers at Birkdale forces the player to really think through how to approach the tee shot. The green is large for a par 3, and pin placements at the upper right of the hole bring all the bunkers into play. If you carry the ball onto the green, it will be difficult to advance it toward that pin. If you miss the green and the bunkers, the chipping area is very similar to one you would experience at Pinehurst No. 2, meaning a challenging chip will follow. On this hole, I hit the best 2 iron I'd ever hit in my life to an inch from going in. I haven't carried a 2 iron in my bag for years, and that shot was probably a gift of the golf gods. Because some mist and fog made it difficult to see the hole, my playing partners thought it went in. They started jumping up and down, but I knew it was short. Indeed, it was less than one ball short of going straight in. I would have traded all my previous four holes in one for a hole-in-one at Birkdale.

Hole 4
Monterey Peninsula Country Club, Dunes Course
Pebble Beach, California
204 yards

The 4th hole at the Dunes Course is a monster, playing 204 yards from the back tees onto the largest green you will find on the course. The tee ground is elevated, and the hole is shaped by dunes on the right and woods on both sides of the hole. A burn shapes the entire green, and 160 yards is needed to clear it. Shots hit poorly to the left or over the green will probably find the burn. Shots flared to the right can find the dunes, which are shaped toward the green. You could get lucky and have the ball ricochet off the dunes and potentially find the green. One extremely difficult pin placement is beyond the dune on the right side of the hole. That back pin position is blind from the tee, but you know it's there. Any shot on the right will find it impossible to get close to that pin. This is a hole where four-putting is possible. My best achievement here was making birdie from the back tee using a driver to bounce through the dunes with enough force to slow the shot as it crawled to within 3 feet of the hole. The 4th is a character builder as it follows the No. 1 handicap hole (No. 3) at the Dunes Course. Your performance on this hole may bear some resemblance to your performance on No. 3 from a confidence point of view.

Hole 5
Pasatiempo Golf Club
Santa Cruz, California
195 yards

The 5th hole at Pasatiempo is another difficult par 3, as it plays longer than its length. The hole is surrounded by bunkers, but there's plenty of green to work with. No matter where the pin is placed, the tee shot must get at least to the middle of the green on the right. Otherwise, the shot might be subject to the severe slope and roll off the green entirely, leaving a very difficult pitch back up to the green and to the pin. The pin positions on this hole are always challenging, especially the pin on the upper left side. Even if you carry the center bunker and land in the left rough, the chip shot will leave very little green to work with. Chips past the hole will roll away significantly from the pin. I feel that this hole has been underrated over the years, but it can be very mean. Not too many birdies will be recorded here. This hole doesn't present a significant challenge to the low-handicap player as ball flight is critical; insufficient ball flight will be very difficult to pull off given the uphill and the bunkering on the hole.

Hole 5
Spyglass Hill Golf Course
Pebble Beach, California
175 yards

You have just endured the first four holes at Spyglass Hill and may be gasping for air, as Spyglass presents a very difficult set of opening holes. You might think things are about to ease up, but the 5th hole is another challenge with another tee shot that has to carry the menacing bunkers that guard the green. The hole plays longer than its yardage, as the tee shot has to carry all the way to the slightly elevated green. The green can be difficult to hold, depending on what the wind is doing. The prevailing wind is normally a crosswind blowing off the ocean. It may tinker with the low handicapper's 7- or 8-iron precision needed to get close to the hole for a birdie. The daily-fee player normally has to hit at least a 5 or 6 iron, which may not hold the green if the shot carries the bunker. This is another hole that has a psychological twist to it, since you have just endured the gut punch of the first four holes.

Hole 6
Riviera Country Club
Pacific Palisades, California
169 yards

The 6th at Riviera is unique, with a pot bunker in the middle of the green. The tee shot must cover the huge donut-shaped bunker in front of the green to have a putt at the back right pin placement. The big risk here is landing the ball on the green and having to maneuver around the pot bunker to get to the hole. At the 2023 Genesis Invitational professional event, Tiger Woods putted the ball into the bunker, which gives you some idea of the difficulty of being short-sighted on this hole. The 6th also offers a significant birdie opportunity by flying the ball to the back of the green on the right, where the hilly slope will accept the shot and release the ball toward the pin. It's all about the position off the tee.

Hole 7
Pebble Beach Golf Links
Pebble Beach, California
107 yards

How can a hole of 107 yards be so famous—or infamous—in the mix of the great par 3 holes in the world? The 7th at Pebble Beach can be the easiest of holes, but it can also wreak havoc on the player when the wind blows. The hole is also downhill to the green, making the distance even shorter than its length. Carved out of the Stillwater Cove, the hole faces the Pacific with a breathtaking view of the horizon. However, club selection is always problematic. Choose a pitching wedge, lob wedge, or sand wedge in "normal" conditions (i.e., no wind or "less wind"). If you can grab the right club at the right time, you should knock the ball onto the green and make no worse than par. Under-clubbing and putting the ball in the front bunker will almost certainly generate a bogey. This hole becomes completely unstable in the wind, as the prevailing wind will blow dead against. When I played Pebble with Arnold Palmer in 2002, the wind on this hole was howling, and we both hit 4 irons. Arnold knocked his shot into the ocean and took a double bogey on his way to shooting 77 for the round. This particular time, I knocked a 4 iron on the green as the wind was blowing close to 40 mph directly in our faces. I made the improbable par.

Hole 8
The Olympic Club, Lake Course
San Francisco, California
185 yards

This hole looks deceptively easy until you arrive at the tee box. The 8th hole at Olympic is entirely uphill, requiring the tee shot to carry all the way to a fairly large green for a par 3. Weather conditions at Olympic's Lake Course are commonly cool and crisp, so the hole will play longer than its yardage. While low-handicap players might hit 6 or 7 irons to this green, the regular player will be hitting a hybrid club or more to try to carry the ball onto this green. Shots that miss the green could end up with some downhill lies in the front bunkers. The rough surrounding the non-bunkered areas around the green is difficult to control because the rough is often moist with dew from fog or brisk conditions. The average player will have trouble with an approach shot from off the green, as they will have to cover the bunkers that surround it. This can be an intimidating shot for the average player, because there's no control of the ball on the green from the rough.

Hole 8
Royal Troon Golf Club
Ayrshire, Scotland
123 yards

The English golf writer, William Park, in *Golf Illustrated*, described the 8th hole at Royal Troon: "A pitching surface skimmed down to the size of a postage stamp." The hole looks rather easy from the tee, and it's hard to imagine that a hole of 123 yards could be as infamous as this one. The tee is elevated, and the shot is played over a gully to a long but narrow green set into the side of a large sandhill. The tee shot must be so precise to avoid the bunkers on either side of the hole. It's almost as if the hole is crowned; a miss to the left or right will invariably find these bunkers. You have to get the ball on the green—no excuses, no deviations—or else. Or else . . . what? These bunkers are horrific, and a miss out of one of them could leave you through the green into the adjacent one. You can hit the ball right to the hole on the front pin position, but if it has any spin it will trickle off the green, avoid the spongy rough, and run right into the bunker just like a missed pinball shot.

Hole 9
Royal Lytham & St. Annes Golf Club
Lancashire, England
164 yards

This picturesque hole looks like it was dropped out of the sky, as it bears no resemblance to what you'd expect at a linksland championship course. The 9th hole seems like a typical par 3 of a parkland golf course, where you imagine that after playing the hole, you could walk into the town just beyond the brush and pick up your dry cleaning. From the tee, the hole appears fairly benign, but from there you can see only three of the nine bunkers that surround the green. The hole is neatly shaped by mounds and brush, and the green is protected by the bunkers. The tee shot must carry the bunkers from every side of the hole to reach the green. From above, the hole resembles an antique rotary phone with the circular placement of the bunkers. The hole can be conquered by a 7 iron, which finds the relatively flat green for most of the pin placements. Wind conditions can make this hole very difficult. Spending time in these greenside bunkers will spoil the scorecard.

Hole 10
Pine Valley Golf Club
Camden County, New Jersey
142 yards

This hole is literally the hole from hell. It's only 142 yards and completely surrounded by sand and evil spirits. You simply can't miss this green. The hole also boasts perhaps the most diabolical bunker on the planet, aptly named the "devil's asshole." Maybe designer George Crump was an astronaut in a prior life and imported this bunker from the moon. If you end up in this bunker, you should probably consider picking up the ball and moving on to the next hole. Of course, I missed the green long with an 8 iron that bounced on the green and headed north to the back bunker; a double bogey 5 was capped off by making a 12-foot putt.

Hole 11
Monterey Peninsula Country Club, Shore Course
Pebble Beach, California
178 yards

The 11th at the MPCC Shore Course appears straightforward, but it's a very well-designed, difficult hole. The tee is elevated, but the downhill advantage is consistently thwarted by the prevailing wind from the ocean—usually in your face and off to the right side of the hole. The distinguishing part of this hole is the size of the green itself, which is essentially a subtle bowl or undulation that pushes shots hit at the pin away from the pin, regardless of where the pin is. I believe it's best to play the tee shot short of the hole and let the ball roll onto the green; pin placements are receptive to this strategy. Carrying the green with the tee shot requires at least a 5 iron, which will be difficult to stop on the green. Low-handicap players can hit 7 or 8 irons onto this green and try to spin the ball toward the pin. The green is completely surrounded by bunkers that eagerly accept most short tee shots, as the opening to the green can't be more than 5 yards wide. Winds can play havoc with tee shots, turning great-looking shots into bunker play. This is a hole that doesn't look difficult but plays exactly the opposite.

Hole 12
Augusta National Golf Club
Augusta, Georgia
155 yards

Golden Bell—Augusta's 12th hole—is one of the most famous golf holes in the world. Entire books have been written about this hole alone. It's been a deciding factor in many Masters events, most recently in 2019 when Tiger Woods was the only player in the final group to avoid the lake. The key to the hole is club selection. The winds at the tee and the winds at the hole seem to be in conflict and confuse the player, resulting in shots that either find the pond (Rae's Creek) or end up long in the flowers and plants over the green. The green is vertical and narrow horizontally, so tee shots must land on the green and stop. For the Sunday pin position on the right side of the green, the pond is clearly in play. Aggressive shots at that pin could find a watery grave and mark the end of the tournament for the player. While Tiger's competitors went for that pin and ended up in the lake, Tiger brilliantly placed his tee shot on the green 30 feet to the left of the pin and two-putted for the par, vaulting him into a lead he never relinquished. One time, I enjoyed making a birdie on this hole, sinking a miraculous 45-foot putt from the top left of the green into that Sunday pin position.

Hole 12
Pebble Beach Golf Links
Pebble Beach, California
200 yards

The 12th hole at Pebble Beach is very underrated, as it's one of the most difficult par-3 holes on the PGA Tour. The tee shot must thread through two large bunkers in front of the green. Players have only a small opening on the right to try running the shot onto the green. The green is also surrounded by thick rough, presenting a difficult pitch shot. The pin placement at the middle right is the kindest and where some birdies are possible. The pin placement at the right rear of the hole is the toughest because it's the least accessible placement. PGA professionals have made some big numbers on this hole. My claim to fame is a birdie during the 2018 AT&T Pro-Am, where I had to hit a 3 wood to that back pin position and nailed it for a net team eagle.

Hole 13
Western Gailes Golf Club
Ayrshire, Scotland
122 yards

How can a hole of only 122 yards be intimidating? This par 3 demands an accurate tee shot, as anything short of the green spells trouble and a potential bogey, or worse, on a hole that looks very easy. At Western Gailes, as at most seaside links courses, winds are a major factor. The 13th hole can play either 150 yards or less than 100 yards, depending on the wind. You must carry the tee shot well onto the green; a ball that just barely lands there may find itself rolling back into the burn that guards the hole, about 25 yards away. The short ball will land and generally release backward into the ditch. This hole reminds me of Augusta's Golden Bell 12th hole in that proper club selection is necessary to get through it unscathed.

Hole 14
Monterey Peninsula Country Club, Dunes Course
Pebble Beach, California
176 yards

The 14th at the Dunes Course at the Monterey Peninsula Country Club is the course's signature hole. It's situated right next to the ocean at the Point Joe turnout on the iconic 17-Mile Drive. You arrive at the automatic gate to access the hole as you cross the Drive and proceed on the path to the back tee. The wind is always blowing here and is always a factor in club selection. You march to the back tee, often with a gallery of spectators who have stopped at Point Joe for views of the ocean. Most of these people don't play golf and don't expect any of us to get near this green. The tee shot has to fly over the rocks in front of you and carry the bunkers that guard the green on the left. Dunes and a well-placed greenside bunker protect the left side of the hole. The prevailing wind is generally off the ocean (right to left), and its strength will determine if more than one club is required to carry everything. I've seen well-struck golf shots lose as much as 40 yards in the wind, ending up sacrificed to the rocks and the ocean. My weapon of choice is always the same: the 7 wood, which I can hit 160 to 185 yards depending on the wind. If the wind moves directly in my face, I have to hit a 3 wood. The hole made national headlines in 2023 when it was almost washed away as ocean swells pummeled the coastline during a string of California's atmospheric river storms. The waves swamped the green and the bunkers and moved some of the boulders that shape the hole. The hole was closed for a few days while the staff hustled to make the necessary repairs, but it was back in play within a few days. Fortunately, the concerned calls and emails I received from all over the country proved unnecessary. Our golf course was not blown away by the storm.

Hole 15
Portmarnock Golf Club
Dublin, Ireland
204 yards

The 15th at Portmarnock, situated on the shore of the Irish Sea, is the signature hole of the course. Views here are spectacular, especially on a brilliant sunny day. The hole is a demanding test. The tee shot has to carry at least 150 yards over the gorse that runs from tee to green and must avoid the two pot bunkers guarding it. Even if you successfully navigate past these hazards, a bad bounce could result in a shot that rolls off either side of the green—which is slightly crowned and can repel certain "good" tee shots. Whenever I've played this hole, the prevailing wind has been predominantly right to left toward the sea. The hole will be very tough against the wind with the tee shot, but you might benefit from gaining more control over the putter on this tricky green.

Hole 16
Cypress Point Club
Pebble Beach, California
242 yards

The "grandaddy" of par 3s is the 16th at Cypress Point Club. Intimidating isn't the right word. This hole is a brute. There's nothing between you on the tee box and the green but the Pacific Ocean. It will take a tee shot of over 200 yards to clear the water. The prevailing wind is usually in your face, which increases your tension of carrying the ocean. There's a bailout area for those who want or need to play this hole for, at best, a bogey 4 by knocking the tee shot about 175 yards to the left of the green. If successful, you'll have an interesting chip of at least 45 to 60 yards to make a par, but a bogey is a good score on this hole from the left bailout area. If the hole plays downwind, you still need plenty of club to get to the green, and the shot has to be high enough to land as softly as possible on it. There's only trouble waiting if you overshoot, as you could find yourself through the green and onto the beach below. I had this experience once hitting a driver long and into the sand. It was low tide, and the ball was sitting up nicely as if a seagull had placed it there. My caddy was encouraging me to play the shot; easy for him to say. All I could do was look up to about 45 feet of natural seawall. I figured it would take a miracle to pull this shot off, but the caddy was persistent. "We got this shot. Just don't take any sand when you hit." I was going to take my double bogey and move out to the penalty area, but the caddy persisted: "You can do this." I climbed down to the beach with my 56-degree sand wedge and looked up at nothing but wall. The caddy said, "Just hit over my head." Miraculously, I did just that, and the ball came to rest about 2 inches from going in for an all-world par 3 on one of the greatest holes on one of the greatest courses on the planet. My sense is that this was a once-in-a-lifetime miracle.

Hole 17
Kiawah Island Golf Resort, The Ocean Course
Kiawah, South Carolina
197 yards

Pete Dye, designer of The Ocean Course at Kiawah Island, created a great closing par 3 hole. The 17th is a long par of 197 yards, completely surrounded by water on the right and well-placed bunkers on the left. The length of the hole and the precision required to hit the green are intimidating features. You have to cross the lake, at least 180 yards, to make it onto the green. Due to the length of the hole, it's difficult to get the ball to stop. Most professionals and low handicappers will be hitting 4 irons or hybrid clubs for the task. Wind is also very much a factor in club selection, as the prevailing wind is off the ocean and sometimes in your face. In a competitive event, the juices will be flowing to get the tee shot onto the green. There's nowhere to bail out here to make par. You can bail out left—similar in concept to the 16th at Cypress—and try to get up and down to make par. But your efforts will most likely result in a bogey or worse.

The hole was made famous by the 1991 Ryder Cup (War by the Shore) in a match between Colin Montgomerie (Europe) and Mark Calcavecchia (USA). Calcavecchia was 2 up (dormie) over Montgomerie as he approached the tee box. Montgomerie promptly hit his tee shot into the water. The match should have been over at that point, as all Calcavecchia had to do was find dry land. Incredibly, Calcavecchia hit a horrible tee shot right into the water as well, wiping out the chance for victory. Montgomerie went on to double bogey the 17th. Calcavecchia missed a 6-footer to make a triple bogey, losing him the hole. He then missed an other putt on 18, giving Montgomerie a halved match. The 17th hole tee shot has haunted Mark Calcavecchia for years, and only Jean Van de Velde's collapse in the Open Championship at Carnoustie was worse than Calcavecchia's tee shot on 17.

Hole 18
Pasatiempo Golf Club
Santa Cruz, California
175 yards

If you designed a golf course with a par 3 for the 18th hole, this is the hole that would silence any critics. This is a truly difficult par 3, with a huge green full of insidious breaks that can bring tears to your eyes after you have four-putted the hole for a double bogey. The tee shot has to carry the barranca that crosses the 10th hole as well. Any tee shot short of the barranca will die in a forest of weeds and brush. It's even worse if you carry the barranca but end up in the cavernous bunker in front of the green. You'll need mountain climbing gear to get down into this bunker and TNT in your sand wedge to carry the ball onto the green. The bunker is so deep that you can't even see the green from inside it.

Tee shots must be as deep onto the green as possible without rolling into the back bunker, as most tee shots will roll back toward the barranca. There's a collection area for tee shots that land on the green but are not deep enough to survive. They roll backwards toward the collection area, requiring a very difficult chip shot to pins that refuse to accept good pitch shots. The left back pin position makes getting near almost impossible, adding at least 10 yards to the tee shot. If you miss it off the green with this pin position into the spinach that surrounds the hole, you will have little to nothing to work with to get up and down from this position.

The green is large and significantly undulated with a variety of pin positions, including one in the middle and one in the left-hand corner, and all very difficult. The hole is gradually eroding toward the chasm at a very slow rate, but tee shots need to be hit past the pin in order to avoid rolling down into the greenside collection area at the bottom of the hole. This is a green with so many undulations that four-putting is always a possibility. No putts are given on this hole in competition, ever.

Despite all of these horribly good design features, I have three of my four career holes-in-one on this hole. The last one was from

150 yards with a 7 iron. I'd just told my playing partners that I had two holes-in-one on this hole and that you had to hit the tee shot past the pin. I knocked a 7 iron straight toward the pin in the middle of the green, flying high and past it. I turned away, satisfied with the shot, as the group started to get excited, seeing that the ball started to release backward toward the hole. It must have taken at least 10 seconds for the ball to travel and clank right in.

17. Yale University Golf Course, 9th Hole

When I was a kid, we lived about a mile from the main Yale University campus in New Haven, Connecticut, in the Wooster Square area. It was populated by New Haven's Italian community and home to some of the best pizza restaurants on the planet. You can ask any Yale graduate to comment on Pepe's Pizza and I'm sure you'll get an excited smile. As an inner-city kid, I spent most of my athletic career on the basketball courts on the streets of New Haven. My main contact with Yale University was working on

Saturday afternoons as a rope guard at Yale Bowl football games, preventing fans from moving from standard seating into the premium reserved section. I played some high school and collegiate basketball at Yale's Payne Whitney Gymnasium. I also won the State of Connecticut free throw championship there in 1965 as a high school junior.

What does all of this have to do with golf? Absolutely nothing. I never held a golf club in my hand until 1973, and it wasn't a pretty sight. I couldn't tell you in 1973 where Yale University Golf Course was. I thought it might be a few miles from Yale Bowl, tucked away in the outskirts of the Westville area of New Haven. This was the upper-crust part of town, and my only experience in that neighborhood was playing CYO (Catholic Youth Organization) basketball at St. Aedan's Church when I was in grammar school.

Fifteen years later, I would have my first experience as a 13 handicapper at Yale. By this time in my life, I had achieved enough financial wherewithal to be a member of a California private club that got me an entry into the hallowed Yale Golf Club grounds in Upper Westville. I was completely intimidated, as my golfing skills were focused on survival and not par or excellence of any kind. Today, with the experience I've had playing all over the world, I can embrace the 9th hole at Yale as a challenge and not a forthcoming nightmare.

The 9th at Yale is a wonderful hole. Although it's quite different from most designs, it shares some similarities with a few other well-crafted holes. The course was designed by the renowned golf course architect Charles Blair Macdonald, with assistance from Seth Raynor.

The 9th is Yale's signature hole, a par 3 that plays from 190 to 230 yards. The green is 65 yards deep with a 5-foot depression that's a product of Macdonald and Raynor's "Biarritz green" design concept. This concept was implemented by the two as they built courses in Europe and the United Kingdom and was applied only to par-3 holes. Other designers have taken the concept further and adapted it to par 4s and par 5s. The Biarritz green has the following features:

- The green is massive, stretching from 60 to 90 yards.
- There's a swale in the middle of the green that's anywhere from 3 to 5 feet deep.
- The green is protected by narrow bunkers on both sides, arranged symmetrically.

Other examples of the Biarritz green concept include the 18th hole at the Old Course at St. Andrews, with its Valley of Sin. I would also add the 16th hole at Pasatiempo, a par 4 designed by Alister MacKenzie, with its huge, triple-tier green with swales that are at least 2 feet deep. The philosophy behind the design was that the player would be tested to hit a long, accurate shot to avoid the swale and hit the green with the pin in the front, or have enough speed for the ball to roll through the swale to the back pin.

The back pin at Yale's 9th measures the hole at 230 yards. To get to it, the tee shot must carry the lake (175 yards) and have enough momentum to roll through the swale to the back pin. There's nothing worse than hitting a great tee shot here that carries the lake but ends up in the swale in the middle of the green. Putting out of the swale is, at best, a roll of the dice. You might relate this putt to a trip through the clown's mouth on your favorite miniature golf layout.

18. The Golden Bell

The Golden Bell, the 155-yard 12th hole at Augusta National, frequently plays a significant role in the outcome of the Masters Tournament. Jack Nicklaus has been quoted saying that Golden Bell is the "toughest tournament hole in golf."

The hole looks fairly simple, just a short iron over Rae's Creek onto a large vertical green. The problem for the player on this hole is club selection. As you move to the teeing area, it looks like you're entering a house of horrors. You have to toss any negative thinking about this shot before you dredge up some of the worst outcomes that might ensue. You look up and try to feel what the wind is doing, and you really can't figure it out. The area seems calm, you pull a club, and the breeze starts to whir through the trees. The breeze triggers doubt in your mind. All of a sudden, what looked like an easy shot becomes a treacherous adventure. You can't be long on this hole or else you'll face a downhill chip out of a bunch of leaves, wood chips, and other paraphernalia. Any mishit could result in a double bogey or worse.

An encyclopedia of disaster greets professionals on this hole. Over a long period of professional play, the average score on The Golden Bell has ranged between 3.05 and 3.56. There's a chronicle of pros who have hit multiple shots into Rae's Creek, a major cause of missed cuts in the Masters.

The 2019 Masters generated complete carnage. Tiger Woods used his experience on this hole to play it to par and eventually win the tournament. The final two groups in 2019 were all in contention as they approached the 12th hole. The pin was placed on the right side of the green over Rae's Creek, the traditional Sunday pin location. Brooks Koepka and Ian Poulter, in the second-to-last group, both proceeded to dunk their shot into Rae's Creek. In both cases, the players went after the pin to try to make birdie, but the winds betrayed the club they selected (probably a 9 iron or pitching wedge).

The final group of Francesco Molinari, Tony Finau, and Tiger Woods showed up after scrambling through the difficult 10th and 11th holes. Molinari held the lead and looked to be in a strong position to win his first Masters. These players had to have known that the preceding group had dunked their shots into Rae's Creek. You might think that this final group would have been sensitized to the travails of the guys in front of them. But my sense is that professional players never think that way, concentrating instead on what they're trying to execute.

Molinari had the honor and promptly went after the pin. The winds swirled, and the ball spun off the green into Rae's Creek. Molinari couldn't believe it; his lead would soon be gone. Finau followed Molinari. After watching Molinari knock it into the creek, you would think he might back off, but he also decided to go at the flag and suffered the same fate as Molinari. Molinari and Finau were flummoxed, but their opportunity to win was essentially over.

Tiger Woods was next. Tiger had won a number of these Masters events and was in the position to win another. He had a lot of experience at Augusta and made the right decision. His goal was to get his ball onto the green and two-putt to leave this golfing chamber of horrors. Woods calmly chose a 9 iron and put the ball on the left side of the hole, leaving him with a long putt for birdie. But this was not the place to attack the course. Woods two-putted and vaulted into the lead in the tournament, eventually claiming the green jacket.

My personal experience with Golden Bell at Augusta National was positive, with three pars and one birdie. Unlike the professionals, I had no experience or preconceptions about what to do on the hole. I knew I had to carry Rae's Creek, but the objective was to get the ball on the green and not worry about anything else. I chose a 6 iron for the 155-yard shot, as that club for me is between 150 and 160 yards. I was prepared to deal with being long, but I didn't want to plunk my ball into the creek.

My playing partners were a bit more aggressive. They chose 8 irons, and one of them experienced the thunderous plop of the ball disturbing Rae's Creek. My birdie was complete luck, and I have my caddy to thank for the opportunity. The pin was in the center of the hole. My tee shot hit the ground just over the green and spun back onto the green some 40 feet from the pin. I managed to hole that putt thanks to the read the caddy gave me. I would have never gotten close without him.

Television will never disclose how difficult and fast these greens are. My putt was downhill, and my caddy told me to hit it at 20 percent speed. Caddies are critical if you're going to enjoy yourself at Augusta.

19. Challenging Holes, 2023 Edition

Hole 1
Augusta National Golf Club
Augusta, Georgia
Par 4
445 yards

Welcome to the Masters! This is the hole where Jack Nicklaus, Gary Player, and Tom Watson kick off the event with their celebratory tee shots. For a player, it can be intimidating—especially for the first-time Masters contestant. The hole has been lengthened from its original 410 yards to 445 yards. It tends to be particularly difficult in colder weather, and the menacing bunker on the right side of the hole is almost a full-shot penalty. Once you get to the top of the hill, the professional will use a medium iron and must carry the front part of this green, as there's a false front that will return short shots back into the fairway about 30 to 40 yards away. Brooks Koepka made a remarkable par in the final round of the 2023 Masters after hitting his tee shot over the trees on the left into the 9th fairway. He faced the entire tree line guarding the hole from 180 yards and nailed an iron shot over all the trees onto the green, escaping with a two-putt par. Most players are not that fortunate, as the stroke average for this hole is 4.24.

Hole 2
Pasatiempo Golf Club
Santa Cruz, California
Par 4
395 yards

The second hole at Pasatiempo is a devilish par 4 that is often overlooked in this unique Alister MacKenzie design. The hole provides a generous fairway that slopes a bit from right to left, which can create some unusual lies. The tee shot is best placed in the center or on the left side of the fairway. There are no easy pin positions on this hole, so the approach shot presents a challenge. The long hitter will have the easiest opportunity with a wedge that has to land in front of the green and release to the pin. The shot requires precision due to all the undulations of the green, which generally push the shot from right to left. The pin position on the left side of the hole is the most challenging; any miss to the left will roll off the green into some gnarly rough that will be almost impossible to convert to a par. The club player generally has anywhere from 150 to 175 yards and will have to approach the green from the opening on the front right side, hoping that the ball will release to the pin. Because the greens are fast, it's unlikely that 5 or 6 iron approach shots will get anywhere near a pin position. The green is surrounded by bunkers, and sand saves here are rare—around 10 percent or lower. Shots out of the bunker will struggle to put the brakes on the ball, making it hard to get close to the pin. You can rack up big numbers on this hole if you miss the green to the right, as the trees will come into play and make pitch shots difficult. Additionally, the approach lane to the hole on the right is cleverly designed to slope slightly upward, causing some chip shots to stall and trickle back onto the fairway. The bottom line: No. 2 looks doable from the tee box, but par is a very good score here.

Hole 3
Monterey Peninsula Country Club, Dunes Course
Pebble Beach, California
Par 4
394 yards

The 3rd at the Dunes Course at MPCC is the No. 1 handicap hole of the course. The hole begins with a very generous, wide fairway, similar to the 2nd hole, but the location of the tee shot in the fairway is important. Depending on the length of the tee shot, the iron shot will have to be accurate because the hole narrows to a small funnel. The green is elevated and completely surrounded by perilous bunkers. A tee shot pulled to the left could find a large fairway bunker that will cost the player a stroke. Shots hit too far to the right can find some scruffy rough that will produce flyer lies, adding to the complexity of the short approach shot to the green. There doesn't seem to be an easy pin position on this green. Especially problematic are pin positions to the back or the right backside of the large green. This green has no level positions; players managing to get shots close are few and far between. It's possible to make some big numbers on this hole; all you need is an errant shot. I would bet that the average score for the membership on this hole is closer to 5.5 than it is to par.

Hole 4
Spyglass Hill Golf Course
Pebble Beach, California
Par 4
350 yards

Spyglass presents a punishing start to the round, forcing you to grind through holes 1 through 4. The 4th is the end of the first phase of the grind. The length of the hole is relatively meaningless. It's a dogleg left, with a fairway that's a vertical spread of green only about 20 yards wide. The entire left side of the hole is beach sand, mounds, scrub, and maybe even the home of a few treacherous creatures. From the tee box, it looks like the dogleg can be cut off by crossing the entire left side, which is about 275 yards to carry. For the ordinary fee player with a decent game, this option is a fool's errand.

The way to play this hole is to knock the tee shot into the fairway for step 1. Club selection is important. Depending on the player's skill, the driver is not an option, but anything from a fairway wood to a long iron will reach the fairway. To set up the approach shot to the green, the tee shot should stay to the far left in the fairway. It's possible, with the wrong club, to drive the ball through the fairway, which will make the approach shot to the green nearly impossible.

A number of years ago, ice plants surrounded the fairway. It's highly unlikely to hit a golf ball more than a few yards out of an ice plant, so my guess is that the Pebble Beach Company received an anonymous message from the golf gods to remove those plants.

If your tee shot finds the beach sand on the left side of the hole, double bogey is probably the best score you can hope for. If you've managed to get the tee shot in the fairway, you are now ready for step 2.

The green on this hole is extremely small, so having a shot of 150 yards or less onto this green is ideal for making par. The green has length but very little width. There's a bunker at the back that's somewhat depressed and can't really be seen from the approach shot. This bunker shouldn't come into play unless the pin is placed at the very back of the green, which, by the way, is a very nasty pin position. Due to the width of the green, missing with the approach shot sets up some very delicate and intricate chip shots that are difficult to execute. There will be birdies made here to reward the successful accomplishment of steps 1 and 2, but my sense is that there are far more "others" recorded on this hole than birdies. The one time I birdied this hole, I considered going on and declaring victory on this golf course. A birdie here feels like a birdie on the 8th hole at Pebble Beach, albeit for far different reasons.

Hole 5
Oakmont Country Club
Pittsburgh, Pennsylvania
Par 4
397 yards

Oakmont is what I would call a "big boy" golf course. You are going to have to bring your "A" game to this venue, as every hole requires precision shot-making, course management, and a good day with the putter. You have arrived at the 5th tee after negotiating and hopefully waving to the Church Pew hazards on the preceding two holes. The tee shot on the 5th is blind and plays uphill, so a drive in the middle of the narrow fairway is critical. Long hitters must be wary of driving the ball over the crest of the hill and potentially into one of the three bunkers on the left side of the fairway. The approach shot should favor the right side of the green, which tends to move from right to left. The approach also has to cover the grassy ditches about 30 yards out. Perhaps they're no issue for the professional or low-handicap player, but the regular player has to be aware of this mess in front of the green. The green is surrounded by bunkers and will be a difficult up and down, especially out of the huge bunker on the right side of the hole. The green is pretty slick, and a number of potential pin positions can lead to some discouraging results.

Hole 6
Royal Birkdale Golf Club
Liverpool, England
Par 4
499 yards

Royal Birkdale is one of the highlights of the Open Championship rota. In this era of the big hitter, Birkdale has strategically placed its fairway bunkers such that the professional player has to really think about whether to take these bunkers on. The 6th at Birkdale is a 499-yard par 4, with the fairway bunker placed at 285 yards; it will take a tee shot of 300 yards to clear it. The hole is a dogleg to the right, with the bunker on the right. The fairway is pretty narrow for a hole of this length, and three pot bunkers guard the front of the large green. A pin placement at the back of the green will make the approach shot difficult, especially in windy conditions. And guess what . . . Birkdale always has windy conditions. Best of luck here. Salute, hope to make par 4, and move on.

Hole 7
Spanish Bay Golf Links
Pebble Beach, California
Par 4
375 yards

While I'm not a big fan of Spanish Bay Golf Links, the 7th hole presents a significant challenge to the daily fee player. Wind can play havoc on this hole, as the prevailing wind is consistently against the player. To have a medium iron to the green, the tee shot requires a drive of 240 yards as close as possible to the middle of the fairway. The left side of the hole is a bed of water reeds—resembling a corn field without the corn—that tends to make the fairway feel narrower than it really is. The right side of the fairway is tempting for the tee shot, but because it's more generous, it makes the hole play longer. The approach shot to the green has to carry the ditch of reeds and scrub, which should not come into play but can impact club selection; any type of mishit will end the round for this golf ball (unless it belongs to Donald Trump). The green is guarded by a large bunker on the right. Unfortunately, it's poorly designed (like many of the greens at Spanish Bay). Although large, its more vertical shape makes it harder to stop medium iron shots. The long hitter loses the advantage because even a perfect drive in front of the gorge will still leave a precise shot of 135 to 140 yards. This is another hole where par is really a good score, and birdies will be few and far between. There just might be as many "others" as there are bogies.

Hole 8
Pebble Beach Golf Links
Pebble Beach, California
Par 4
385 yards

The 8th hole at Pebble is not only hard—it also combines its difficulty with awesome beauty. The hole is one of the most intimidating in golf for the average player and a good challenge for the professional or low handicapper. The tee shot is blind from the back tee, with only a stone marker to give you some indication of where you should be hitting the ball. Professionals and low handicappers have to hit a shot as close to the end of the fairway as they dare. The fairway ends at a deep cliff over the Pacific Ocean, with breathtaking scenery to the green below on the other side of the gorge. The second shot is all carry to the green with little room for error on either side of the hole.

At the 2021 AT&T Pro-Am, Jordan Spieth's tee shot trickled through the fairway and ended up in a precarious spot. Spieth decided to hit a shot to the green from a position that could have cost him his life. I believe his caddy wanted him to take a drop, but Spieth had enough confidence to assess the situation and his safety, pulling off an incredible shot across the chasm to the green. The green has a series of very difficult pin positions. A par here is the norm on what is surely one of the most difficult holes on the PGA Tour.

The 8th hole was the "waterloo" for a number of players during the 2023 US Women's Open. The hole was played from the men's championship tees, and with the wind blowing into their faces, many of the players could not get their tee shots into position to carry the chasm over the Pacific Ocean below. Irish amateur Aine Donegan was the first-round leader and was 3 under par for the tournament in the third round. Her approach shot to the green in the face of the wind failed to carry the gorge. After going back to the drop zone, her next attempt suffered a similar fate, eventually recording a 9 for the hole—moving her from -3 to +6. This hole would essentially cost her low amateur status as she finished second to the low amateur by one stroke. The world's then No. 2 player, Nelly Korda, could only hit her tee shot 154 yards and suffered a similar fate as she had 240 yards to the hole—a bit too much to ask for as her ball careened into the rocks below. Lexi Thompson, who is one of the longest hitters on the LPGA Tour, could not navigate the chasm and became yet another victim of this tough hole.

The daily fee player will have a difficult time with this hole. The tee shot has to be long enough on the left side of the fairway so that the player can hit a hybrid or long iron across the gorge to the green—or to a position close enough to the green for an approach chip shot. It's not worth talking about any shot that's hit to the right, as it will find a watery grave.

My last experience here was notable for my ego. I was playing in a charity tournament with Andy Miller (Johnny Miller's son), who was also a PGA Tour player. After coming off the 7th green nearby, Johnny Miller showed up in his golf cart as he was roaming around the course talking to the players. I've known Johnny for years and felt a little pressure coming to the tee box with him watching. I then proceeded to hit with my driver the best tee shot I have ever hit on this hole, reaching the professional end of the fairway along with Andy. Johnny clapped as I completed my swing. Coming from him, this was something I will not forget. It's great to execute a shot in front of a legend.

Hole 8
Monterey Peninsula Country Club, Shore Course
Pebble Beach, California
Par 4
410 yards

The par-4, 8th hole on the Shore Course at the Monterey Peninsula Country Club is not as intimidating as Pebble's 8th. Still, the hole is the No. 1 handicap hole on the course, and you'll need all of your skill to make a par here. The hole is a dogleg to the left that poses a problem for the long hitter and the average club player alike. At the right angle of the dogleg, at approximately 220 yards, sits a monstrous tree. Fairway bunkers crouch at the foot of the tree and extend another 20 yards down the left side. The prevailing wind is normally in your face, adding a few yards to the fork of the dogleg. The long hitter has a choice to make: a driver might send the ball through the fairway and into the fescue off to the side. Alternatively, if the tee shot is left of the tree in the fairway, there's an opening for an educated fade with a long wood or hybrid. The average player's approach shot has to cover the tree. There are also bunkers on the right that shouldn't come into play for the long hitter.

This is not a hole for a missed shot, as strokes will begin to multiply. The green is immense, so the approach shot must be accurate to avoid the dreaded three putt. The 8th hole is really a wake-up call; up to this point, the Shore Course has laid everything out in front of you, and you're able to understand the approach shots that are required. On the 8th, all bets are off, and you'll need a variety of shots and options to make par. This is a good par for the low handicapper. The tee shot and wind conditions make club selection difficult, and there is also the huge green to contend with. The long hitter has to decide whether to hit a driver or 3 wood, as a drive through the dogleg will not end well. The player who can hit a draw 300 yards will have a flip wedge to the green. If that draw is short or too long, trouble awaits from the bunker and the gnarly bushes that frame the hole.

Hole 9
Kauri Cliffs Golf Course
Northland, New Zealand
Par 4
350 yards

Kauri Cliffs is another gem in New Zealand owned by the same company that developed Cape Kidnappers, one of my favorite courses anywhere. While there are a number of spectacular holes at Kauri, where the ocean is in view for fifteen of the eighteen holes, I found the short par 4, 9th hole particularly difficult, as it plays longer than its yardage. From tee to green, there are three platforms in the fairway, all heading uphill. The tee shot needs to find the fairway; I don't believe there's much chance of recovering from the hay-type rough on the left or the bunker on the right. The fairway slants a bit from the left toward the bunker, so a good tee shot should be center-left and past that right bunker. The approach shot should be a short or medium iron to a very large green surrounded by bunkers. The green slopes a bit from left to right, and the best play is to be below the hole to have a putt at a birdie. Kauri has several holes where you can avoid the grind and get rewarded for good shots, but the uphill platforms of this hole demand a high degree of difficulty. Par is a good score here.

Hole 10
Pebble Beach Golf Course
Pebble Beach, California
Par 4
450 yards

When you play Pebble Beach, the first seven holes of the course are gettable, with birdies and pars as realistic opportunities. You then arrive at the 8th hole and find that the next three holes are all very difficult and can be quite intimidating. The 10th, the last of these difficult holes, might be the hardest one, but there's not much in it. I would rate 8, 9, and 10 at Pebble all as a 10 on a difficulty scale of 1 to 10. The 10th hole plays right along the Pacific Ocean on the right, in a similar grind—almost as a continuation—of the equally difficult 9th hole. The tee shot should be center-right of the fairway to set up a medium iron for the long hitter and a long iron for the daily fee player. The left side of the green is guarded by a massive bunker and a morass of scrub. All putts on the fairly small green will break toward the ocean. The key to this difficult hole is two excellent, accurate shots to get as close to this green as possible, as any errant shot will produce some very big numbers.

Hole 11
Pasatiempo Golf Club
Santa Cruz, California

In my previous book, *Through the Green*, I described the 11th hole at Pasatiempo as the hardest 11th hole I will ever play. It still qualifies for that honor. I decided to include the following hole at Chambers Bay in the current list of the hardest holes.

Hole 11
Chambers Bay Golf Club
University Place, Washington
Par 4
425 yards

Chambers Bay was designed by Pete Dye and became a controversial U.S. Open venue in 2014. The course is walking-only, with no cart traffic, and is at least a 7- to 8-mile trek. The links along the Columbia River and railroad tracks provide a quaint and gentle backdrop for what is a pretty tough golf course. The 11th hole is a good example. It winds around to the left, almost a dogleg, and the tee shot has to carry 200 yards to reach the narrow fairway over the sand and brush. There's a bunker about 225 yards out from the tee that you can't see from the tee box. Players face trouble on both sides of the hole, but the worst is the series of bunkers on the right side. I managed to drive the ball into that hidden bunker and then, to my amazement, proceeded to hit my best shot of 2023: a 7 wood out of the bunker to 20 feet on the right side of the green, where I made a two-putt par. Quite gratifying and the highlight of a very satisfying day at Chambers Bay.

Hole 12
Winged Foot Golf Club, West Course
Mamaroneck, New York
Par 5
633 yards

The recently installed championship tee at Winged Foot is set at 633 yards and plays at least 550 yards for the members, so it's all-you-can-eat on this hole. Iconic Winged Foot boasts a membership that reputedly has the most single-digit handicappers of any club in the United States. The 12th hole is a straightaway with a pretty narrow fairway for a par 5 of this length. There's a fairway bunker at 339 yards that not too many professionals would take on—besides someone like Rory McIlroy. The interesting part of the fairway is that it slopes to the right off a ridge, such that a tee shot in the right-center of the fairway could end up in some punitive rough. Any miss to the left will find a similar fate. As a result of the ridge, the professional has only about 17 yards of fairway width to land in for a potential shot at the green. Mere mortals will require three or maybe four shots to the green, as the fairways at Winged Foot don't run very much. Four bunkers guard the entrance to the green, with three additional fairway bunkers ready to catch second or third shots. These bunkers share real estate with the 17th fairway. This is certainly a strong par 5 and perhaps a par 6 for the regular club member.

Hole 13
Monterey Peninsula Golf Club, Shore Course
Pebble Beach, California
Par 4
375 yards

This 13th is one of the most difficult holes on the Monterey Peninsula Shore Course at 375 yards from the back tees. The hole probably has more bunker area than fairway. The tee shot looks a bit like the 4th hole at Pebble Beach, requiring players to carry the first set of bunkers, positioned right in the middle of the fairway, about 175 yards off the tee. The bunkers meander to both sides of the fairway, so the best tee shot is center-left. The fairway funnels to the green, narrowing to only about 10 yards wide at 50 yards into the green. The second shot is to another very large green, which can add a club depending on the pin position. The hole is right off the ocean, so expect wind to play a factor for the approach shot to the large green. The bunker on the left receives a preponderance of approach shots due to the narrow entryway to the green. The green is so large that the only accessible pin position is the front pin. If the shot moves past this pin position, the putt back is downhill and is a low-probability effort. Other pin positions also present significant difficulty for getting the ball close, with a number of undulations and breaks on the green that measure at least 11 on the stimpmeter. Par is a very good score on this hole, especially if the pin position is at the back of the green.

Hole 14
Friar's Head Golf Club
Baiting Hollow, New York
Par 5
509 yards

Friar's Head is another gem along the coast of Long Island, New York. It has a wonderful feel of links golf. On a number of holes, you'll have to hit accurate tee shots to position your approach shots to the green, maneuvering around a sea of bunkers, fescue, and other types of rough stuff. I never thought that a hole could resemble the 18th at the Shore Course at Monterey Peninsula Golf Club, but the 14th at Friar's has some amazing similarities.

The 18th at Monterey is a par 4, while the 14th at Friar's is a par 5. The similarity is the tee shot, where both holes have a huge bunker to carry on the right side to attack the hole. The bunker at the 14th at Friar's is 225 yards from the tee, but it will take a 240-yard accurate tee shot to carry it. The second shot (same as Monterey) is significantly uphill, requiring a highly accurate shot to the green, which is surrounded completely by bunkers. Any approach shot past the hole that ends up in one of these bunkers is likely to have a very difficult downhill bunker shot. Also, like Monterey, the right side of the 14th is shaped with trees and some branches guarding the green. The green is more elevated at Friar's, and the huge bunker in front has to be covered. Monterey has an annoying hump in the middle of the green that rejects some very good approach shots which the 14th does not have. Monterey's 18th green has a bit of a backstop, enabling the player to approach the shot past the pin and spin it back toward the hole. The 14th is a better design than the Shore Course hole, giving the player more options to attack the hole without poor, unpredictable results. The 14th at Friar's gives me some ideas for redesigning the 18th at Monterey.

Hole 15
Cape Kidnappers Golf Course
Hawke's Bay, New Zealand
Par 5
661 yards

Cape Kidnappers is the most breathtaking golf course that I have ever played. I believe the 15th hole, named Pirate's Plank, is the signature hole of this Tom Doak masterpiece. It's the type of hole you can't stop photographing. The fairway is very wide for the tee shot but continues to narrow as you approach the green. The second shot must be in the fairway, as the hole is carved out of a cliff; any shots that miss the fairway right or left will not be gettable (not even a Trump ball). The approach shot to the green will depend on the length of the first two shots, but it should generally be between 100 and 150 yards to a green that is perched 150 yards above the sea. You will not be able to fly this green, as the ball will end up in the Pacific Ocean. I found the approach shot to be intimidating, especially when trying to get the ball close to the pin. You have a tremendous feeling of desolation because there's nothing between that green and the ocean, 150 yards below. It's an intoxicating experience.

Hole 16
Shinnecock Golf Club
Long Island, New York
Par 5
616 yards

The most difficult par 4 I have ever played is the 16th at Pasatiempo in Santa Cruz, California. I have covered this hole like a blanket in my prior books, so I've chosen a different links hole that is a par 5 but just as difficult as Pasatiempo's par 4. The 16th hole at Shinnecock is a monster for the amateur and a good test for the professional.

Shinnecock has hosted a number of major championships, most recently the U.S. Open in 2018. For the professionals, the key variable in determining whether this green is reachable in two shots will be the wind. The tee shot has to carry 300 yards to clear the first set of bunkers and 351 yards to run through the fairway into a morass of gorse and other evil plants. The second shot will have to cover 265 to 280 yards to reach a fairly narrow green, which is on the small side.

The rest of us mortals will have to hit a tee shot 220 to 240 yards to the right side of the hole to reach the fairway and avoid the first set of bunkers. The second shot will have to be accurate and clear the bunkers and gorse to the right, landing on the right side of the fairway for an approach shot of at least 150 yards and up to 180 yards, depending on the wind. The hole is visually intimidating, and you don't want to land anywhere other than the fairway as there is nothing but bunkers, gorse, and other sources of bad lies that will significantly impair an approach shot off the fairway. There must be at least twenty bunkers on this hole, and errant shots will produce large numbers on the scorecard. The narrow green slopes back to front, creating several difficult pin positions. Par is possible here as well as the probability of the dreaded "other."

Hole 17
Royal Dornoch Golf Club
Dornoch, Scotland
Par 4
405 yards

Royal Dornoch is a bucket list venue for any golfer. You get an uplifting feeling about the place as soon as you arrive. It's a feeling that is quite different from the Old Course at St. Andrews or Pebble Beach Golf Club. It's a mysterious sensation of understated exuberance. You finally made it here after all the scheduling nightmares, and starting your round is seamless and easy. The course and location are everything you thought they would be. It has all the characteristics of an outstanding links course, with views of the Dornoch Firth.

The 17th hole is an outstanding design and provides the penultimate challenge for the round. The tee shot is blind, with directional poles, as the target is about 240 yards in the distance. The key elements in playing this hole are position off the tee and the uncontrollable nature of the wind, which is almost always present. There are two bunkers on the left side of the hole, which will come into play with an offline tee shot. The left side also has gorse bushes that must be avoided. The best play is driving the ball into the middle of the fairway, then taking a medium iron to hit an approach shot to land in the valley. This strategy will not yield a green in regulation, but you will have a clean wedge or less for a shot up to the elevated green for a par attempt or a two-putt bogey. This strategy may not yield a birdie or a par, but it will leave you with a sigh of relief that you have navigated this tough hole in one piece. The long hitter has to drive the ball straight into the valley—not exactly simple, with significant trouble if the shot is wayward. A successful tee shot into the valley will take the sting out of this hole, assuming that the wind doesn't wreak havoc on an approach shot if the wrong club is selected.

Hole 18
Whistling Straits Golf Club
Kohler, Wisconsin
Par 4
520 yards

The 18th at Whistling Straits is a fitting finish to a wonderful round of gulf on the shores of Lake Michigan. For the long hitter, the temptation is to knock the tee shot at least 285 to 290 yards—over what seems to be a vast number of bunkers on the left side—to get to a slice of fairway for an approach shot of at least 170 yards to the green. This tactic is high risk and high reward, since missing the fairway here will eliminate any opportunity for par or even bogey. If you're playing the hole as a par 5, the best play is to stripe the ball down the middle of the fairway. The next shot will be a long one and require laser-like precision to avoid the horrendous bunkers that dominate the left side of the hole. You probably can't get to the green this way, but you will have a 50- to 60-yard approach to the green for a par putt. It's very important to get the second shot into the right position for an approach shot to the green. The hole is infamous for Dustin Johnson failing to realize that the pile of sand on the right side of the fairway was actually a bunker. Spectators had also been standing in the spot, so the site was significantly trampled down. Johnson grounded his club, finished the hole, and was assessed a penalty stroke for his play in the "non-bunker."

20. The Worst Designed Golf Holes

In my mind, the worst holes of all time have the following design flaws:

- Blind tee shots
- Blind water hazards that are not visible from the fairway
- Trees in the middle of the fairway
- Long carries to reach the fairway from the tee
- Fairways that are completely uphill where the green isn't visible from the fairway
- Humps in the middle of the green where approach shots can't hold their landing spot on the green

In the following list, I present the worst holes in order, starting with the "worstest." These holes represent the poorest qualities of design and playability. Amazingly, they are often surrounded by some of the best golf holes in the world, which makes their awfulness stand out even more. Great examples of this type of hole are the 18th at Cypress Point and the 18th on the Shore Course at Monterey Peninsula Country Club. Golf pundits would probably label my criticism as blasphemy, but I think you would get a sheepish nod of agreement from those players who have had the good fortune of playing at these venues.

Hole 18
Spanish Bay Golf Links
Pebble Beach, California
Par 5
516 yards

This hole wins the prize for being the worst-designed hole on the planet, and the worst I have ever experienced because it's terrible for players of all levels. It has absolutely no redeeming qualities and should be redesigned into a par 4 of, say, 450 yards. The tee shot requires hitting to the right side of the fairway; anything to the left will face a mound with nothing but a waste area beyond it. The width of the fairway to maneuver this tee shot is narrow for a par 5, as there is scrub and rough all the way up the right side.

The second shot is straightforward, provided you're in the fairway, to hit a wood or long iron straight down the fairway. At this point, the approach shot to the green is a complete right angle to the left. There is no place to go left of the green because this side of the hole is replete with swamp and rough. The green is huge and horizontal, and the approach shot will be across a sea of sludge, muck, and bunkers. Depending on the quality of the second shot, the approach to the green could be 120 to 160 yards to carry the mess in the front. Approach shots hit through the green will be punished with sticky rough surrounding a green that has lumps and humps all over it.

The hole is particularly ridiculous for the mid to high handicapper, and any shot on this hole that isn't perfect will probably eliminate any chance of par. I don't believe the low handicapper has a chance to reach this green in two, and the hole takes away the length advantage. I would convert this hole into a 450 yard par 4 by relocating the green to the end of the fairway and eliminating the ridiculous right-angle approach shot. I would also add a bit more fairway for the tee shot by removing some of the rough on the right side. This hole will never be a good par 5 and is a terrible end to what is a pretty good golf course. After playing this hole, you can only walk away with the idea that the designer had to have been restricted by the environmental requirements of the property. This is the worst golf hole on the planet, and almost every player I've spoken to about this hole agrees.

Hole 13
Blackwolf Run, River Course
Kohler, Wisconsin
Par 3
150 yards

Tall Timber, the 13th at Blackwolf Run's River Course, is another terribly designed hole—close to the worst I've seen. It is patently ridiculous. Its name comes from the trees that guard the entire right side of the hole. The tee shot has to carry the trees to get to a large green for a par 3 that is generally horizontal. While this hole might be "a piece of cake" for the low-handicap or professional player, it's impossible for a high handicapper—who has to hit a shot from 150 yards that must be at least 75 feet airborne for 100 yards. If you decide to play away from the trees, there's a huge bunker to greet that shot, or you will have a putt of 60 to 70 feet. Designer Pete Dye must have had a bad night before he woke up and put this one on the drawing board—one of the most ridiculous golf holes I have ever seen.

Hole 18
Blackwolf Run, River Course
Kohler, Wisconsin
Par 4
510 yards

The 18th hole at the River Course of Blackwolf Run is a tough finishing hole due to its length, and it's visually difficult if you haven't played the course before. The tee shot has to carry a large depression on the right that can't be seen from the tee box. You might think you have a decent tee shot to the right only to find the ball in the middle of this depression. From this position, you have a blind shot to the green and really have no choice but to keep the ball to the right to set up a wedge shot in hopes of getting up and down for a par. If you miss the hole on the left, you are likely to find the greenside bunker, making par a very difficult task. My objection to the design is that the depression on the right simply isn't necessary to preserve the integrity of a strong hole. It my opinion, it's not a good design.

Hole 1
San Jose Country Club
San Jose, California
Par 4
310 yards

San Jose Country Club is one of the oldest clubs in the Bay Area and has a number of outstanding members and alumni, including the great player and TV golf analyst Roger Maltbie. The course has some excellent holes, especially on the back nine from fifteen on in. The course has immense possibilities, but the club needs to acquire more land to open things up on the front nine. (For comparison, par on the front nine is 33, with 37 on the back nine.) The opening holes at San Jose are rather disappointing, starting with the 1st. The hole has little to no character as it is a drive straight up a hill to the smallest green on the course. The opening tee shot is generous, with trees on the right that will come into play only with a bad slice. The second shot will be a short club for all players to this small green, which will not hold a shot even though most players will be hitting wedges. Shots to the green have to be extremely precise to hold with spin; any bounce will pull the ball to the back or over the green, and the pitch back out of spiny rough is difficult to control. You can make birdies on this hole, and you can also make "other" if you miss the green or end up in the huge front bunker that punishes shots when the distance has been misjudged. I'm at a loss as to how I would redesign this hole, since there is no room to do much of anything. It could be redesigned into a very difficult par 3 by moving the tee box up by 35 yards, but that would reduce the front nine to a par 32, which isn't really a good idea for the course.

Hole 9
Stanford University Golf Club
Palo Alto, California
Par 4
365 yards

My Stanford friends would wince at the mention of their venerable golf course having a candidate for the "worst" holes I have ever played. The front nine at Stanford isn't the most wonderful layout; I would rate it slightly "north" of a typical public venue. But the 9th is particularly poor and can be mastered only by the low-handicap player, in my view. It seems like the designer ran out of land to complete the front nine. The 9th hole follows the pleasant par 3, 8th hole, which is one of the best holes on Stanford's frontside. You arrive at the 9th tee box and see a fairway that is no more than 20 yards wide, which will intimidate the medium- and high-handicap player. There's no escape, as any ball that misses the fairway is probably lost to jungle on the right or gravel on the left. The drive has to be in the fairway and at least 215 yards down the middle. The low handicapper will probably hit an iron off the tee to ensure the ball lands in the fairway.

It gets worse, even if you're in the fairway, as you now have a steep uphill shot of at least 170 yards to a green that slopes severely from right to left. Slow play is a big problem at Stanford because any university student can play the course. It's run like a private club but actually operates as a municipal jungle, with rounds taking at least 5 hours or more. The 9th is the worst hole on the course, but the good news is that the course design from 10th through 18th is actually wonderful. The 9th conjures up thoughts of Pasatiempo's 7th hole. It has a similar fairway width, except that missing right or left on the 7th will hit a tree, and there's a shot back into the fairway. When you miss the fairway at Stanford's 9th, you reach into your bag for a new pellet.

Hole 18
Cypress Point Golf Club
Pebble Beach, California
Par 4
365 yards

At Cypress, you get to play one of the best courses on the planet for the first seventeen holes. When you reach the finishing hole, you have to wonder what they were thinking. The hole is a dogleg to the right up a hill that isn't especially steep, but is lined with a number of trees close to the middle of the fairway. There's an excellent chance that your straight tee shot will hit or ricochet off one of those trees, in which case, you can say goodbye to making par on the hole. The hole makes no sense to me, and the best thing is to aim directly at the trees and hope for the best. This hole is really a "head-scratcher" for such a spectacular venue.

Worst Golf Courses

There are also entire golf courses that could land on the worst list by being virtually impossible to play irrespective of your handicap. Such a course is the Friendly Hills Golf Club in Whittier, California, which makes my list as one of the worst I have ever played. I'm sure that the membership of Friendly Hills would not appreciate this designation, but Friendly Hills is actually a misnomer; it should be called Unfriendly Hills. The course is short but extremely narrow and hilly, and any missed shots can compound into more difficulty. It really doesn't matter if you're a long or short hitter off the tee shot, the course will punish you either way. I suppose as a member you would eventually figure out a way to play it well enough to achieve a reasonable score, but based on my experience, I would not be pursuing a second chance at this venue.

While the Friendly Hills Golf Club is an unfriendly golfing venue, the worst of the worst is Poppy Hills in Pebble Beach, California. My saying this is golf course blasphemy at its highest level, as Poppy is the home course of the Northern California

Golf Association, so it doesn't get much public criticism. At one time, Poppy was one of three courses in the rotation for the AT&T Pro-Am tournament. The professionals hated the course; the term "trash pit" was heard in the professional locker room during the event. Poppy was eventually removed from the rotation and replaced by the Shore Course at Monterey Peninsula Country Club.

Poppy's original design was so poor that it was almost immediately redesigned after it opened. Most golfers would not agree with my assessment, but Poppy will never make a top 100 list. I have read reviews praising Poppy as an experience similar to Augusta National or other famous venues. I'm at a loss to understand how Poppy can get these positive reviews, but my opinion will not waver that this is the worst course on the Monterey Peninsula and one of the worst for a destination venue in the country.

The course is boring. You hit the ball as far as you can and stay out of the tree line. There's no rough, and it's difficult to determine where certain shots should be hit to reach the green. It plays long, as the fairways do not move the ball because local conditions are generally moist and/or breezy. Even after the renovation, you can still get bad bounces to good shots, which will end up in potentially horrible places, including out-of-bounds.

I find the greens to be inconsistent in speed and pace. Some of the greens are downright ridiculous, looking more like the clown shot at the local miniature golf course. I hate the 18th hole, which most people state is the signature hole, due to the undulations, junk, and bunkers surrounding the green on a long par 5.

I do like the 1st hole, which is a strong par 5 that provides a generous fairway with bunkering in the right places. The pond on the left side of the hole can come into play for the second shot if it's pulled because the middle part of the fairway slopes toward the pond. It's the beginning of many of Poppy Hill's poor design features, but the pond adds attractiveness to the hole.

UK Golf

I've played golf in the UK many times during my life. No matter which courses I play or how many times I return, it seems there's always something new and different to enjoy. Here, I've assembled a few stories from trips to England and Scotland that I think demonstrate the range of experiences possible in that part of the world.

21. Somerset, England Golf

My response to the San Francisco Bay Area heat dome in 2022 was to simply leave the area. In July, and again on Labor Day, I flew to stay with my close friends, the Shirleys, at their home in the Somerset area in the southwest of England.

I have visited Somerset and my friends Brian and Jacky Shirley frequently over the years. Somerset is a very nice part of the world, approximately 100 miles from Central London. It's a farming community dotted with quaint villages and a few famous places including Stonehenge, the town of Wells with its picturesque Anglican cathedral, and the cities of Bath and Bristol in the northern part of the county.

Every time I come to England, something big seems to happen. That July in 2022, they sacked the Prime Minister for lying. If we did that in the United States, we wouldn't even have a government.

Then I arrived again in September, and the new Prime Minister took office, had her first session in Parliament, went to get the Queen's blessing at Balmoral Palace—and two days later, the Queen died. The country was plunged into mourning, making transportation around the place more difficult.

However, there were a few positives. One, the weather was great, with bouts of rain, clouds, and sun mixed together with a high temperature of 75. Two, food at the Shirleys is like eating at a 5-star restaurant all the time. And three, golf.

Golf in Somerset is a pastime pursued by all ages and, in my experience, has an informality and welcoming atmosphere while adhering to the Rules of Golf and the etiquette required. As in many other places around the world, the pandemic revived the popularity of golf among millennials here, and investments in golf and course redesign have recently proliferated. Two courses come to mind as good examples of the general environment for golf in the region.

Long Sutton Golf Club
Langford, Somerset
Par 72

Long Sutton is a course located in Langport, which is a tiny hamlet among many in Somerset. The course seemed a bit strange to me, as almost every hole is a dogleg to the right or left, except the par 3s. I have never seen so many dogleg holes on a golf course. It makes for challenging play, because the course length from the regular tees is about 6,400 yards. There are also a number of burns to carry from the fairway, making local knowledge a requirement to get the yardages right to cross these penalty areas.

The fairways are generous; the tee shots have to be placed in areas where the green can be addressed from the fairways. The course doesn't have the feel of a traditional parkland-type English or Irish course, yet it's still difficult due to its length. You don't really grind through this course, but you have to hit shots to the right positions to attack the greens. Despite the plethora of dog-legs, the holes do give off different looks. The challenge becomes personal: hitting the right shot to the right position. The various burns and ponds always get your attention, but a good player won't be stressed about the challenge—it's a matter of executing the shots.

Wheathill Golf Club
Lovington, Somerset
Par 68

For twenty years, I kept a set of TaylorMade irons, putter, and woods at the Shirleys'. When I gave those clubs to their 16-year-old Scottish nephew, it gave me the opportunity to buy a new set of Titleist irons and woods—the same as I play with in California, except they came with standard steel shafts (no composite).

While Brian cradled the latest technology driver of choice—the TaylorMade Stealth—he bequeathed me his 20-year-old 9.5-degree TaylorMade driver, which I love. I bought a brand-new Odyssey putter, which I had to buy again in California, as I found I was making everything in Somerset with that putter. Despite the strong dollar and weak pound exchange rate, all this stuff cost about 50 percent more than in the U.S. Thankfully, this array of tools prepared me for playing Brian's private club: Wheathill Golf Club.

Wheathill is a course nestled in the Somerset hills with gener-ous views, situated amidst a sea of greenery punctuated with dairy farms and related businesses. What's interesting about Wheathill is that it's a course that's uniquely suited to players of all skill lev-els, including people learning to play golf. It's also a great place for good players to practice different shots from all types of distances to sharpen their game, and for medium to high handicappers. It's a course without stress, yet it presents enough challenge to try to score well.

The course is only 5,800 yards as a par 68. Despite its short length compared to today's typical layouts, which measure between 6,200 and 7,500 yards, Wheathill offers some very interesting holes to challenge players' skills. The fairways are broad, and the bunkering is fairly straightforward for the average golfer. I found Wheathill to be harder than a typical resort course style of layout that you might experience in Hawaii. The course's best defense mechanisms are the burns that run through a number of holes. The burns crisscross various fairways on the course and are positioned to be in play. A good example is the 4th hole, a par 4 where the burn is only 30 yards from the green. An iron shot coming onto this green must be hit high enough to cross the burn and hold the green.

The 3rd hole is the strongest on the course and the number-one handicap hole. It's a 408-yard dogleg to the left, also protected by a burn some 50 yards from the green. The hole has a wide fairway, but if the tee shot isn't long enough (say 235 yards), the approach shot will be a long iron that brings the burn into play and makes it difficult to hold the green.

The 6th hole is another strong hole requiring accuracy off the tee. The tee shot has to carry another burn at 170 yards, but the hole is a slight dogleg to the right. The tee shot is unusually narrow here, and players must avoid a tree to the left of the tee at 100 yards to get the ball into the middle of the fairway. Once the burn is crossed, a comfortable iron shot to the green is possible to make par or better.

The 9th hole is a rambling par 5 of 488 yards that's wide open for the tee shot, but slightly uphill and blind toward the green. A well-executed second shot will put the player into position to have a shot of 100 yards or less downhill to the green for a birdie opportunity. Many players can get to this green in two if the tee shot is long enough, because the last 80 yards or so are on a downhill slope. It also depends on course conditions; the ball may be running or not depending on the state of the fairway. There are many days when bouts of intermittent rain showers can slow ball speed through the fairway.

Another fun hole is the par 4, 13th of 362 yards. It has a tree in the middle of the fairway where the tee shot might land and another huge tree guarding the right side of the hole for an approach shot from that right side.

The best tee shot is to the left of the tree at 210 yards or so; a tee shot to the right, even if it's in the fairway, brings the tree into play for the approach. The margin for error on the left isn't great, so if the tee shot is pulled left, there's enough heather and rough to make the approach potentially more difficult. The hole reminds me of Stanford University golf course's 12th, which also has a large tree in the middle of the fairway. Stanford's fairway is a bit wider, and there's nothing guarding the green, but its green is a lot larger and surrounded by bunkers.

My favorite hole at Wheathill is the 16th. It's a 480-yard par 5 that can be birdied but can also yield some really bad outcomes for errant shots. Visually, it's a lovely hole that meanders to the left. It has two sets of hedgerows that must be carried, almost like the walls at North Berwick. The first set of hedgerows is only 100 yards from the tee, but the position of the tee shot has to be left-center to get a possible shot to the green. The farther the tee shot goes to the right, the longer the hole becomes.

The second shot has to carry the next set of hedgerows, and the yardage for this shot is completely dictated by the length of the tee shot. The second set of hedgerows is only about 150 yards from the green. Depending on where you are in the fairway, you might want to hit a shot just up to the hedgerows to leave yourself a 7 iron-type shot to the green. Long hitters will have a good chance of getting to the green in two, but the green is small for a par 5, and second shots may not be able to hold it.

Low points at Wheathill are the 1st and 18th holes, which are nondescript and not worthy of much comment. It looks like the course ran out of real estate for both of these holes. For the 18th, especially, designing a new finishing hole would add some shine to this little jewel of a course. But my take is that it's a project that probably isn't economically viable.

The greens at Wheathill are the weakest part of the course. Compared to the quality of Long Sutton, it's almost like night and day. The green conditions are probably the result of cost issues for the club, as they are decently designed but not fast, even in dry conditions. Bottom line is that playing Wheathill is fun and uplifting. If you hit good shots, you will be rewarded. There is no grinding at Wheathill.

22. Royal Birkdale Golf Club

Royal Birkdale Golf Club is an absolute gem and is one of the few golf courses that hasn't required lengthening or streamlining for the modern game. Located on the northwest coast of England, Birkdale is part of the regular Open Championship rota and hosted the 146th championship.

Birkdale Golf Club was founded on July 30, 1889. The subscription price to join the club back then was equivalent to about $1.50, and the green fee was about $0.50. The first course was nine holes and was constructed for about $7. I'm sure construction didn't entail any earth-moving equipment other than a few shovels. Perhaps the only thing necessary to complete construction was placing some metal flags in the holes. The club was officially opened on October 5, 1889. Ladies were able to play three days per week and have always held a prominent role in the operation of the club.

In 1908, eighteen holes were measured, with drainage completed the following year. Golfers would no longer have to play in their wellies (rubber boots). In 1922, the club tried to buy the links but could not come up with the necessary $21,000. The land was sold to the Southport Corporation, and the owners offered a 99-year lease to the golf club. The clubhouse was completed in 1935.

The Open Championship was scheduled to be played at Birkdale in 1940, but there was a global conflict going on at the time called World War II, and the area was being continuously bombed by the Germans. The first Open Championship was held at Birkdale in 1954. Three years earlier, in 1951, the King of England had bestowed the title "Royal" on the club, and it became the Royal Birkdale Golf Club.

It's interesting that an Englishman has never won the Open Championship at Birkdale. The winners are:

- 1951: Peter Thomson (Australia)
- 1961: Arnold Palmer (U.S.)
- 1965: Peter Thomson (Australia)
- 1971: Lee Trevino (U.S.)
- 1976: Johnny Miller (U.S.)
- 1983: Tom Watson (U.S.)
- 1991: Ian Baker-Finch (Australia)
- 1998: Mark O'Meara (U.S.)

In the 1961 event, Arnold Palmer drove the ball under a small bush on the 15th hole (now the 16th). At a critical point in the championship, Palmer chose to go for the green from under that bush, which was, at best, impossible. He smashed a 6 iron out from under the bush onto the green to preserve his lead. The shot was so implausible that the spot of the shot is marked by a plaque to commemorate his feat.

In 1969, the Ryder Cup was held at Birkdale. The competition ended in a tie when Jack Nicklaus conceded a putt to Tony Jacklin to halve their match, thus ending the competition in a 12–12 tie. The conceded putt has been memorialized as a significant achievement in sportsmanship aptly named, "The Concession."

My great experience at Birkdale was a close call at a hole-in-one on the 206-yard par 3, 4th hole with a 2 iron. It was the best 2 iron I had ever hit in my life, and the group on the tee was convinced that it was "in" and were very excited. Although I couldn't see the ball from the tee, I was reserving my own excitement—which turned out to be justified. The ball lie was about 1/4" over the hole, but the wind was blowing in the wrong direction for it to drop in. After 10 seconds of prayer, I settled for a tap-in birdie 2. It would have been the highlight of my golfing career if that ball had gone in. My birdie 2 is not famous or even important, but it was still an unforgettable moment for me.

23. Richmond Golf Club

Richmond is a parkland golf course in the southwestern part of London. You have to know exactly where it is, as there are no markings or directions to the course. You drive down to the end of a private lane through what looks like a castle entry. As you cross the 18th hole roadway into the parking lot, you need to stop before proceeding into the club to ensure that no approach shots are in the air seeking the 18th green.

As you pass through this unusual entry to the club, you'll see the majestic clubhouse that adjoins the road to the right of the closing hole. The clubhouse is a national historic site built in 1725. Sudbrook House is an imposing classical structure and an example of 18th century Palladian architecture. Most UK clubs are cluttered with annoying signage and warnings surrounding their clubhouses, sporting inane instructions about what you can and can't do. You won't find any of this at Richmond, as it would certainly spoil the ambiance of the place and detract from the scenic views of the clubhouse.

The golf course is a par 70, and at 6,100 yards, is pretty short by today's standards. The course is a good test, fair but not difficult. Weather conditions will dictate how challenging the course will play, and wind, rain, and fog can always interrupt the daily pattern in the UK. Nick Price, winner of three major championships and a former World No. 1 in the mid-1990s, holds the course record with a round of 60.

TEMPORARY
WARTIME GOLF RULES

1. Players are asked to collect Bomb and Shrapnel splinters to save these causing damage to the Mowing Machines.

2. In Competitions, during gunfire or while bombs are falling, playes may take cover without penalty for ceasing play.

3. The positions of known delayed action bombs are marked by red flags at a reasonably, but not guaranteed, safe distance therefrom.

4. Shrapnel and/or bomb splinters on the Fairways, or in Bunkers within a club's length of a ball, may be moved without penalty, and no penalty shall be incurred if a ball is thereby caused to move accidentally.

5. A ball moved by enemy action may be replaced, or if lost or destoryed, a ball may be dropped not nearer the hole without penalty.

6. A ball lying in a crater may be lifted and dropped not nearer the hole, preserving the line to the hole, without penalty.

7. A player whose stroke is affected by the simultaneous explosion of a bomb may play another ball from the same place. Penalty one stroke.

RICHMOND GOLF CLUB
SURREY, ENGLAND
1940

While Richmond is a tidy golf course and very interesting to play, it holds a special badge of honor. Being pretty close to Heathrow Airport, the course was bombed by the Germans in World War II. The war didn't stop the members from playing, though, so to adapt to a unique set of course conditions, the club adopted the following rules:

The 18th hole is a nice way to finish. It has a generous fairway that leaves a second shot into a very small green surrounded by well-placed bunkering. It's a hole that looks easy but ranks right there with the 18th at the St. Andrews Old Course and North Berwick. Richmond is a very entertaining track. It looks easy, but you had better pay attention to the subtleties of the course, which can jump up to bite at any time.

24. Royal St. Georges

The weekend was going to be special: three days of golf in Sandwich, in the south of England. The weather forecast was promising, but in England, you never really know. It was April, so there was a decent chance we might escape the usual unpredictability of the British climate. But no guarantee.

Brian Shirley and I left Saturday morning for an afternoon tee time at our first venue, the Royal Cinque Ports Golf Club in Deal, Kent. The three-hour drive down from London was pretty simple, and we were excited for our three-day weekend of golf. We left Brian's house around 9 a.m., expecting to get to Kent by noon with plenty of time for our 1:30 p.m. tee time. We pulled into the car park where it all starts, at a British private golf club, where visitors are clearly viewed as outsiders and, as the Japanese would say, "gaijin" (foreigners).

Car parks are littered with placards that tell you where you can park, what you can wear, slow play rules, and on and on. Royal Cinque Ports (also known as Deal) in Kent was a standard bearer for the British private (members only) club. Brian and I had enough experience with all of this nonsense, so we proceeded to the pro shop to sign in and maybe hit some practice balls to warm up. This is when the fun began.

Brian sauntered up to the assistant professional to sign us in and pay the green fee for our round. Brian whipped out his credit card, and the professional stated, "We don't accept credit cards for payment of green fees." With a startled look on his face and slightly embarrassed, Brian then pulled out one of his business cards and asked the professional to please bill his business for the green fee. The professional looked at Brian as if he was from the planet Mars: "We don't do that here."

Brian knew that this was customary throughout England and was incredulous at the attitude of the professional—so rude and unwelcoming. The pro stared blankly at Brian with a stale and stoic demeanor and said, "We only accept cash for green fees." Brian was clearly livid and stated that he didn't have that much cash on him; we probably needed about 300 pounds sterling to cover the cost. Big-shot expatriate American had no sterling in the wallet, only U.S. dollars.

"Well, now what?" Brian asked the pro.

He replied, "I can't really help you."

"Does this mean that we can't play this afternoon? My friend here is from America, and he came all the way over here to play this course in Kent."

He remained aloof and unmoved, and our only option was for Brian to drive into town and use his ATM card to get the cash to pay the green fee. I'm really helpful here . . . I didn't have an ATM card, and I still don't even have one today (I'm actually proud of this). Brian looked at his watch and knew that it would be close to tee time by the time he returned with the cash.

I was dumbfounded by the behavior of this club professional. We had never had an experience like this in all of our time playing golf throughout the UK. Brian made it to town and back and paid the fee. The professional barely acknowledged his presence and what he had gone through to obtain the necessary cash. There would be no warm-up, and we would be fortunate to make it to the first tee. The final chapter of this heinous event is the coup de grâce.

We headed out to the 1st tee and toward the championship tee box so we could play the course at about 6,700 yards. What happened next was really unexpected. The entire pro shop staff, including the head professional, came flying out of the pro shop as if the place had been hit by a World War II Luftwaffe ordnance. They were motoring out of that pro shop as fast as they could to protect what??? They all ran up to us as if to arrest us for grand larceny, screaming, "You cannot use the championship tees; they can only be used for competitions and only for the members." Wow, I thought, these guys have a few loose screws; we obeyed them and moved up to the gentler "tees of the day." But on the 2nd hole, out of the sight of the pro shop, we went back to the championship tees for the rest of the way. The course was okay but seemed very ordinary. It didn't make a lasting impression on either of us, apart from how we were treated.

Royal Cinque Ports had a parting shot for us, though. We couldn't use the bar or the restaurant, as we didn't have a jacket and tie. Our nerves were shot at the end of this round, and things could only look up from here.

Day 2 was Sunday, and things started nicely with brilliant sunshine offsetting the gray clouds and drizzle of our "wonderful" day in the gloom at Royal Cinque Ports. One thing was for sure, we couldn't be treated any worse at Prince's Golf Club than we'd been treated at RCP.

We arrived for our early afternoon tee time, and it just seemed right away that things were going to be different. Many of the members had been out playing in the morning and were now joining their families for lunch on the veranda or dining room. Prince's demonstrated a sense of calm, happiness, and general welcoming, in contrast to the indignities of the preceding day.

Prince's has twenty-seven holes, and we played two of the nines: Himalaya and Prince. The pro shop had no trouble accepting Brian's credit card for the green fee, and we proceeded to play on a day that was as calm as the demeanor of the staff. We were actually treated like customers. What a concept! Prince's had hosted the Open Championship in 1932 won by the legendary Gene Sarazen. The wonderful British commentator and former professional Peter Alliss was a member and had made some changes to the course in 1985.

Brian and I played stress-free golf in unseasonably prime conditions of sunshine, warmth, and little to no wind. No excuses, and we both scored in the 70s.

Day 3, Monday, would be the day we came here for. The opportunity to play Royal St. George's (RSG) would be a real treat, but we didn't know what to expect. After our Dr. Jekyll/Mr. Hyde experience the previous weekend, we had some trepidation about what might be in store for us as we appeared for our early-morning tee time at RSG.

The weather was actually the median of the two earlier days: the cool, wind, and grey skies at Royal Cinque Ports and the warm, sunny, and blue skies at Prince's. Today it was patches of grey and blue skies, wind, and bouts of warmth and cold throughout the round at RSG. Great conditions to play an Open Championship venue, along with spectacular views of the sea.

Given the previous weekend, we didn't know what to expect when we went into the pro shop. It was quiet that morning. We were the only players going out early, as we would be driving back to London after the round.

The head professional greeted us warmly, and immediately, the stress of our expectations ran completely out of our system. He encouraged us and stated that the course was in fine shape and ready for us to take on. We asked about any restrictions and he chuckled and stated, "Go out and have a good time." "What about tees?" we inquired, and the professional said, "Play whatever tees you like and play well." He certainly need not apply for a job at Cinque Ports.

We were psyched and started off playing pretty well. I hate to get off to a troubled start, especially on a course like this, and things went smoothly. We navigated the tricky par 3, 3rd hole, but off to our right, we could see the 4th and a huge bunker off in the distance. It was distracting, and I almost started to fear what was coming next.

We got to the 4th tee and our jaws dropped seeing what was in front of us. Although we weren't going to play this hole from the championship tee, it was easily an "all carry" 230-yard tee shot into the wind over a bunker that could have been designed only by the devil himself or herself, depending on your gender preference for Beelzebub. There was no choice except to drive the ball over this Himalaya bunker, as there is nothing but deep rough on both sides of the hole. Your drive either found the fairway or you were going to make an "other" on this hole.

Brian calmly stepped up to the tee and smacked the drive about 250 yards over the bunker onto the fairway—he hoped—as the fairway is completely blind from the tee. It was now my turn. I gulped and hit one of the best tee shots in my golfing career, sailing over the bunker and landing—I hoped—in the fairway. We trudged up the hill, in prayer, and behold, both shots had found the green grass known as the Elysian Fields.

We had conquered the Himalaya bunker and waved it good-bye. After a couple of long iron shots of 180 yards, we both found the green and two-putted for pars and breathed a huge sigh of relief. I was happy just to have conquered the bunker; anything else was a cherry on top of the sundae. This was the best drive I had ever hit in England, bettering my near miss for a hole-in-one at Royal Birkdale.

We both played well in deafening and peaceful silence throughout the round, with Saint George's presenting a number of interesting challenges along the way. Brian was the better man that day, but the experience was terrific and worth the entire trip, as memories of the prior two days instantly faded away.

The 4th hole, for our skill level, was probably the most intimidating piece of real estate we had ever encountered in our golfing careers. The character of RSG is truly differentiated with its array of challenging holes, spectacular scenery, distinguished flags (cross of St. George), and thatched roof shelters to protect you from the vagaries of the wind and rain that often accompany playing links golf by the sea.

Playing St. George's seems to be like getting the best parts of all the other great venues in England, Scotland, and Ireland. The fairways and heather remind me of Royal Portmarnock in Ireland. The solitude and quiet by the sea remind me of playing Royal Troon, where all we could hear was an occasional whir of

a military jet landing at Prestwick Airport. I think the Himalaya bunker ranks pretty close in penalty to the Road Hole bunker at St. Andrews.

The Open Championship returned to Royal St. George's in 2021 after a ten year hiatus following Darren Clarke's 2011 championship win. RSG has hosted the Open fourteen times, which is more than any other venue in England. It's puzzling why it took so long to bring the Open Championship back to Sandwich. The course brings the entire professional field into play, not just those guys that bomb the ball. I remember John Daly hitting a 380-yard drive on one of the par 4s at the 1993 Open, which was won by Greg Norman. The field is wide open; witness the 2003 championship by the relatively unknown Ben Curtis.

The professionals have to think their way around this course, where the 7,200 yards are challenging only if the coastal breezes become a factor in the event. Collin Morikawa won the 2021 Open, becoming the first player to win on his Open Championship debut since Ben Curtis in 2003. Subtle changes were made to the course for the championship, but I enjoy seeing the guys pump it 292 yards over the Himalaya on the 4th hole. In the last Open Championship, the average score on number 4 was 4.50.

25. North Berwick—A Very Special Place

North Berwick is a tidy seaside town in East Lothian, Scotland, situated on the south shore of the Firth of Forth. The quaint village, well-appointed homes, and comfortable hotels remind me of Carmel, California. North Berwick is known for being where the aristocracy of Edinburgh either come to vacation or have a second home. The town has direct, convenient rail service from Edinburgh.

While the rest of the world was sweltering in record heat, our visit to North Berwick in 2023 was a bit warmer than normal for the locals but very comfortable compared to the intense heat plaguing the rest of Europe, with London experiencing its highest temperature in recorded history at 104 degrees.

For American golfers, North Berwick remains a relatively unknown gem, primarily because the course has never hosted an Open Championship. This distinctive course reminds me of a number of venues unrelated to links golf courses. The 1st hole evokes the 1st hole at St. Andrews, with its generous fairway and the Firth of Forth on the right side of the green, ensuring any slice here will be out of bounds.

North Berwick is noteworthy for the variety of holes, each one special in its own way. After the short par 4, 1st hole, the 2nd hole is a 433-yard par 4 with the beach in play all down the right side. Fortunately, the front nine was playing downwind during our round, so the 2nd played considerably shorter, and we avoided the beach.

The 3rd hole presents a wall that cuts across the fairway. After a tee shot down the middle of the fairway, my 3 wood was hit well but not high enough, and it careened off the wall with a dull thud—leaving me with a 170-yard shot that I executed reasonably well for a 2 putt bogey.

The 6th hole (Quarry) has a huge bunker guarding the front of the green that must be avoided to survive continuation of play. The 7th (Eli Burn) is a 366-yard par 4 that presents the first burn on the course, with three deep bunkers guarding the green.

We closed the front nine with two challenging par 5s, including the 8th (Linkhouse) with its eleven bunkers. Playing the front nine downwind was a pleasant experience. You felt that if you made good swings, you would get good results and avoid most, if not all, of the bunkers.

The back nine, however, was against the wind. As we turned to begin, the wind picked up, and the grind was on. The course was clearly going to be more challenging as the wind started changing directions, sometimes against and sometimes crossing from the ocean to inland, right to left.

The Firth of Forth was on our left for the entire trip to the clubhouse. We had to aim tee shots toward the rough and the sea to make the fairway, because any shot down the middle would end up in the right rough or worse.

The 10th hole (Eastward Ho), a 172-yard par 3, is reasonably straightforward, but you have to play away from the bunkers. The 11th hole (Bos N Lockers) is a 549-yard par 5 that played 650 yards on this day, with a huge bunker on the right side of the fairway.

The fun isn't really supposed to start until the 13th hole. But things got more difficult as we approached the 12th, with the wind gaining intensity. The 402-yard 12th hole is a dogleg left with four bunkers on the left and a bunch of gnarly rough. I wasn't going to hit many greens on the back nine, so the idea was to keep the ball in the fairway and hit the "war-torn" gap wedge 65 yards every time. The gap wedge, which has been my best offensive move against the winds throughout our Scottish venues, would serve me well for the holes to come.

The 13th hole (Pit) was my favorite. It's 400 yards, and the green is small and guarded 50 yards out by another wall. My playing partners, all big sticks, ended up carrying the green and going over into the rough, where they faced some difficult downhill chip shots. My 65-yard gap wedge came through again as I hit my third shot over the wall to 8 feet, then I holed the putt for a very satisfying par.

The 14th (Perfection) is aptly named as it requires perfect technique against the howling winds that made the hole play at least 450 yards. The shots on this hole are completely blind; your aim is the directional pole that sits behind the green above the

beach, where you will end up if you get anywhere near that pole. The prevailing wind blows hard from right to left. Significant cross bunkers on the right instantly reminded me of the huge bunker at No. 4 at Royal St. Georges. You simply had to carry these bunkers or else.

The 15th, the Redan hole, is a 190-yard par 3. "Redan" is a French military term for a fortification formed as a U-shaped embankment toward the expected point of attack. I don't know much about military strategy, but this hole was well fortified with horrendous bunkers, especially around the front of the green. There was no way that my ball flight with a hybrid or 3 wood was going to carry these bunkers against the wind. I decided to hit a driver and let the wind do whatever it decided to do, as I wanted to avoid the bunkers. The strategy worked, but my drive slipped off the green far right. I was then unable to get up and down for par, but a bogey generated a sign of relief. Anything landing in those bunkers would have been a scorecard killer.

We then proceeded to the famous 16th hole (Gate). Members and patrons of North Berwick say that Gate is a hole that you will either love or hate. I would say hate is the appropriate term for this round; however, I would get another chance a few years later, at which point the hate turned to love.

The tee shot is interesting, as you must cross a burn that is similar to the 17th hole at Carnoustie. But on this day, the burn was 205 yards out against the wind. I decided to lay up to the burn and play the hole conservatively, like I had done at thirteen and fourteen.

I didn't execute the gap wedge well on the approach shot, though. The shot peeled off the green to a horrible position that required chipping uphill—an extreme version of Pinehurst No. 2. The green is immense. An indifferent chip led to a three-putt and a painful double bogey (Hate).

My latest try at the hole yielded a wonderful chip shot to 6 feet, and a drained putt yielded a great par (Love).

The last bout of punishment occurred on the 17th, another long par 4 dotted with bunkers and trouble. But we were coming down the mountain of difficulty.

I absolutely loved the 18th hole, which bears a strong resemblance to the 18th at St. Andrews. A wide fairway leads to the clubhouse at 277 yards with a prevailing "with" wind. I should have made birdie here as my 50-yard wedge came to rest 5 feet from the hole. Alas, I missed the putt, closing the day with a routine par that culminated a wonderful experience.

26. A Scottish Odyssey

On June 1, 2024, sixteen players affiliated with the Pebble Beach Golf Club arrived in Edinburgh, Scotland, to commence an odyssey that would cover five golfing venues. The players ranged in ages from mid-40s to 85!

The trip had been professionally arranged six months earlier with secured tee times, hotel reservations, and dedicated transportation services. Players were coming in from everywhere on various flights with various degrees of difficulty. One set of golf clubs coming in from Toronto, Canada, never made it, and this predicament became the first major story of the event.

With the group finally assembled in Edinburgh, we set off for a 5-hour bus ride to Royal Dornoch Golf Club. We stopped roughly halfway at Pitlochry, a small town well positioned geographically as a hub for tour buses traveling to various points of interest all over Scotland. The tour buses empty their passengers to shop, eat, and stroll in this rustic town.

The town gobbled up the tourist trade, and its streets this Sunday afternoon were teeming with locals being joined by numbers of bus patrons descending on the fish & chips shops, bars, restaurants, and mom-and-pop retail shops charging London-type prices. It seems like all that was needed were a few slot machines, and Pitlochry could become the Las Vegas of Scotland.

After a fair meal and a trip to the loo (cost 50 pence), we re-boarded our bus for the rest of the trip. We arrived at about 6 p.m. at the Dornoch Station hotel, a short stroll to the Royal Dornoch Golf Club where we would play on Monday and Tuesday. In our group, we had four players who were determined to play whenever possible. There would be no waiting for Monday. With 5 hours of daylight left in the Scottish sun, they were off to Dornoch for as many holes as they could get in.

The Dornoch Station had recently been renovated and looked very cozy, comfy, and well-appointed. The staff were prepared for our arrival, and everything was looking great until I walked into my room. It was the smallest hotel room I had seen in years. I had to go back in memory to the airport hotels near Narita Airport in Japan to recall being in a room this painfully small. There were no drawers or cabinets anywhere to store or hang clothing. The bathroom had no storage or any place to set toiletries, so I placed my toothbrush and toothpaste on the base of the television. It was amazing to me that a hotel that had been so nicely refurbished and modernized could have gotten its rooms this wrong. I would certainly be living out of a suitcase, literally, for the next three nights. But this is what can happen on the road, so you just "suck it up" and consider the great golf course you are about to play.

After our one member's golf clubs did not arrive in Edinburgh from his direct flight from Toronto, the chase was on to figure out how and when to retrieve these clubs. The handoff from the airline to a local messenger service would prove to be quite dodgy, unpredictable, and frustrating, as once the airline delivered the clubs to the carrier, communication with the owner became a black hole.

The purchase of an AirTag on the golf bag proved invaluable, as finally, the clubs could be tracked inside the carrier's vehicle. They were at last delivered on Monday evening. The victim in this affair played out of my bag on Monday, and he putted so well with my putter that I had to keep a close eye on it for the rest of the trip.

Dornoch Round and Match

We played Dornoch on Monday as a warm-up for a match on Tuesday against the Royal Dornoch club, to be followed by a dinner with their members at the clubhouse. We moved to the 1st tee, which is a friendly, welcoming hole that I would name "Benign." It's a short hole with very little difficulty, but you quickly realize that this is just a welcoming appetizer. You immediately move to the 2nd hole, which I would label "Jolt." It's a par 3 of 170 yards, which is all carry to the green, or you get the mounding effect of a Redan. It's not quite a Redan, but it's close, and missing the green is not a good thing.

The next three holes are strong par 4s, with their fairways sloping from right to left and multiple fairway bunkers eager to swallow a well-struck tee shot. These holes are primarily played downwind, which gives you the false sense of security that you can defy the presence of these bunkers. However, it seems that these holes were designed with the prevailing wind in mind, so avoiding the bunkers was a challenge.

The par 3, 6th hole looks appetizing, but any wind miscalculation, and you could end up over the green to a very uncertain fate. I was a big fan of the 7th hole, as the wind is directly at your back. A short hitter (as I am) could not hope to cover 492 yards in two, but this is exactly what happened on both days. The last two holes on the front nine are extremely difficult and reminded me of the Pacific Dunes course at Bandon Dunes, as these holes are by the sea.

The 9th to me is a replica of the 12th at Bandon Dunes, but I'm pretty sure that Dornoch predates that design. The hole plays steeply uphill with a bifurcated fairway and the ocean directly on the left. A tee shot hit down the middle or middle/left could find the rough on the left—or worse—as the rough on this hole is wispy. A tee shot hit down the middle or middle/right will hold its line for a shot to the green. With the wind in your face and the uphill slope of the hole, the second shot is long and critical. I grabbed a 3 wood and smashed it down the middle of the fairway on the right side. All of my playing partners saw the shot and thought the ball would be very close to the green. We never found the ball! I couldn't believe it: the best-struck ball of the round, and directionally sound, could not be found. It was maddening, and I had to swallow some emotion over having to take a lost ball penalty that spoiled two great shots.

I needed a Mars bar at the turn to calm down, and one of the sympathetic members insisted on buying me a mini bottle of local Scotch (Royal Dornoch brand). It was the first time I can remember ever swigging a shot of Scotch while playing, but it had a positive effect. However, the short 10th surrounded by bunkers would set the tone for the rest of the round—a difficult grind.

The back nine holes offer high risk/reward. To claim par, they require the proper placement of tee shots to avoid the patches of rough on some narrow fairways. The 14th hole is a long par 4 without any bunkers. Still, it's the No. 1 handicap hole, with the prevailing wind in your face and a number of grass mounds on the right. The 14th is intimidating, absolutely requiring an accurate tee shot because this hole demands two solid strikes in the right place. The second shot from the fairway must carry the mounds on the right that guard entry to the green, although they are at least 40 to 50 yards away from it. Some players will lay up to the mounds and chip over them to try to make a one-putt par.

The green, sitting atop a gentle slope, seems to be situated as an altar in the cathedral. The precision required on this hole is a 10 on the 1 to 10 scale of survival. After the difficult 14th, you might think you'll find relief on the shortest par 4, 15th, but the wind can lengthen this hole to 400 yards of golf. There's a mound 20 feet wide on the left of the hole, but I chose to fly all of it to the left with a hybrid club. The wind carried it over, but I got up and down from there with a two-putt par.

My favorite hole at Dornoch is the 17th. The first time I played it in 2022, the wind was directly in my face, and it seemed impossible. This time I made par as the wind was present but not penal. The hole has two fairways, with the left one offering the long hitter the best option to have a reasonable iron shot onto the green. The green is blind from the tee with a directional pole indicating the bifurcation of the fairways. The short hitter has to play to the right fairway—and hit it accurately in that fairway—to position for a shot to the green of at least 180 yards. My drive was in the right fairway but too far back to go for the green, so I laid up with a 7 iron, where I could try to get up and down from 60 or 70 yards. I clipped a gap wedge up the hill past the pin and slammed a putt from about 10 feet for an unlikely par. It's difficult to describe how entertaining this hole is with the two fairways, scrub in front of the green, and the size of the green. It is truly a unique design. The 18th is another strong par 4 finishing hole demanding two great shots to close out a remarkable piece of God's earth.

The match against Royal Dornoch presented a special treat, allowing us to meet the members and soak in the culture of the club. The results of that match were not disclosed (probably in deference to us), but I'm sure that the home club won. The dinner was a classy affair; I think it might be only the second time I donned a coat and tie all year. The members were thirsty for information about U.S. golf and Pebble Beach in particular.

Dornoch has a long waiting list for club membership, but unlike the U.S., the coming-in fee is hundreds of pounds as opposed to hundreds of thousands in the U.S., particularly in California. Dornoch would be the toughest course we would play on this trip, but it was a glorious experience. The course delivers a punch but will also reward at the same time.

St. Andrews

On day 4, we packed up and headed south for another 4-hour bus ride to the Old Course Hotel in St. Andrews—and yes, another pit stop in Pitlochry. The Old Course Hotel is home of the Old Course at St. Andrews, and you might instantly compare it to the Pebble Beach Lodge, home of the Pebble Beach Golf Club.

For me, the comparison ends there, as the Old Course Hotel

demonstrated a consistent, customer-oriented experience completely focused on golf and the logistics and infrastructure required for a great stay. We were able to unpack our stuff in these sumptuous rooms and not worry about a thing. The breakfast room at the Old Course is first-rate and the best I have experienced on the road.

On Thursday, we descended on Kingsbarns Golf Links for a late tee time that would take us until 8 p.m. with plenty of brightness to spare. The course was in wonderful condition, with well-manicured fairways and a very attractive layout, allowing us to use all the clubs in our bags. Kingsbarns was a delight to play. It had any number of challenging holes but did not require the precision of playing a course like Dornoch. It would be untrue to state that it was an easy course, because you had to place your shots in the right places to have the scoring opportunities. It just seemed that there was more clarity on what you needed to do without the feeling of grinding through negative thoughts. It was all in front of you to execute.

The most difficult hole, in my view, was the 15th, which can be described as wicked and extremely intimidating. The hole is a par 3 of 180 yards, where the ball simply has to be in a straight line or slightly center-left. Any shot that deviates from this line could be potentially "dead." The left side of the hole is completely sculpted by trees; any shot that is pulled off the tee is gone. The right side of the hole runs along the ocean from tee to green, so any shot that fades will also be completely dead. The hole extends to the right, meaning a faded shot would have to carry 200 yards to hit the green and could bounce farther right into the ocean.

The hole gives you a sniff memory of the 16th at Cypress for the intimidation factor, although Cypress is a sterner challenge, having to carry the ocean straightaway. The 18th at Kingsbarns is a fair hole but really difficult into the wind. It's a great finishing hole, especially if it's downwind, as you get to play over the burn onto the green. The burn is very much in play, and it was a pleasure to hit this green in regulation and leave with a pleasant memory of a very well-designed course.

The par 3, 8th hole played for us at only 120 yards, but the

8th HOLE

design of the hole is delightfully diabolical. The green is large horizontally but not vertically. The pin was placed on the left side of the hole where the green slopes severely from right to left. The ideal shot is to hit the green at the point where it slopes such that the ball will release to the left toward the hole. Our group managed to make a few birdies here by hitting the ball in the right place. A less precise shot could hit the right side of the green and roll off into some ugly rough, making par a desperate possibility.

The Round at the Old Course

The next test would be the Old Course at St. Andrews. We turned up for our tee time at 2:30 p.m. to find a welcoming starter infrastructure and local caddies that would prove to be out-standing during this round. There was only one small problem: the bright sunshine and pleasant temperatures were offset by a 25-mph wind with gusts up to 40 mph. Oh well, we're here and we're doing it, so off we went.

I always thought the 1st hole was easy. It has the widest fairway on the planet, over the greenside burn onto the green for an easy par. Easy? Not today! The 1st hole was right into the teeth of the wind and was probably playing 450 yards. My tee shot wasn't par-ticularly great, and I had no shot to the green. I ended up hitting a 7 iron from 110 yards to 6 feet. I got that par, but the grind was on.

On the par 4, 4th hole, I had 150 yards left into the wind for what was effectively a 175-yard shot and knocked it to within 4 feet for an unlikely par. However, my competitor in the match holed out with a wedge from 80 yards after nearly hitting his tee shot out of play for a birdie 3. Such is the game of golf. We ended up making an easy par on the downwind par 3, 8th hole, and I drove the 9th hole—all downwind.

The bad breaks came on 7th and 11th where I ended up in Shell bunker after the wind killed what I thought were good shots. I labored heavily in Shell as there was very little sand in the bunker because the wind was blowing it around. It felt like trying to get out of a hole that had just been bombed.

Usually, the sand in these bunkers is fine and soft, so if you can control your backswing tempo, you can get the lift required to extricate the ball from the bunker and pull off a decent shot. In this particular bunker, however, the sand behaved like gravel, and it was hard to control my swing tempo. I was determined to get out of this bunker, but between the gravelly sand and my ball sitting at the base of a 5-foot wall, it took three attempts to get it out and onto the green.

After a great bogey on 16th to square our match, my playing partners all attacked the Road Hole (17th) and drove the ball over the hotel into the fairway. The Road Hole is one of the most in-timidating holes in golf, bounded by the bunker on the left and a wall on the right. I hit the straightest drive of the day down the middle, which is really a no-no as I had at least 175 yards to play a shot almost 90 degrees back to the fairway for an approach to the green. I used a hybrid club to get to the green and got down in 3 for a well-earned bogey.

We crossed the Swilcan bridge, posed for the requisite photo, and moved to the iconic 18th hole. The tee shots were great thanks to the assist from the wind, and I cleared the path for an easy pitching wedge to the green. Avoiding the Valley of Sin, the ball fell to the back of the green past the hole, where I executed a pedestrian 2-putt par to close out a tough but great day at the home of golf.

The caddies did a phenomenal job guiding us around this terrific layout, and the Shell bunker episode was my only failure on the day. I had managed to avoid every other famous bunker on this course, but I now own the Shell bunker badge of futility.

North Berwick Golf Club

It was on to North Berwick for the final chapter of this Scottish golfing odyssey. We pulled up to the Marine Hotel in North Berwick in the late afternoon, and once again, a group decided to head out to play at Gullane just down the road. I was saving my last bit of energy for the North Berwick links, my second time playing there. I had taken the weekend off from playing to give my back and knees the rest they needed so I could walk the course.

Monday morning dawned with brilliant sunshine, moderate temperatures, and an average wind, and I began to relish the opportunity that would arrive at our 3 p.m. tee time. We headed over to the course at about 2:15 p.m. to the same conditions, found our caddies, and took the tee.

As soon as the group stood on the first tee, the sky turned gray, the wind started to howl, and the rain began to pour. I couldn't believe it as now my rain gear was safely tucked away in my golf bag back at the hotel. I was completely exposed and started to get wet. For some unknown reason, my level of focus and concentration seemed to heighten. I cracked a 4 iron onto the first green and made par. In 2022, I can remember making double bogey on the 1st after a poor tee shot. It seemed like the more the rain came down and the wetter I got, the better I played. At least I had the good fortune of having rain gloves in the bag.

I was even par after the 6th and chipped in a shot after punching out of a bunker sideways. It finally stopped raining, but the wind continued to howl, which had a drying effect on my clothes. The rest of the round was played without the rain. Compared to my 2022 round, this one was significantly different. In 2022, the back nine played into a furious wind, which forced you to grind through these difficult holes. On this day, the wind swirled around in all directions, which made shots easier to understand—not necessarily easy, but you were more in control of the situation.

We approached the famous 14th Redan hole, a par 3 of 190 yards of pure hell. This time, the wind was behind us, so I had the luxury of taking a hybrid club, which I hit perfectly, leaving me with a 100-foot putt on the green. No matter, I made the green, whereas in 2022, I couldn't reach the hole against the wind with a driver. Once again, thanks to some great caddies, we managed to avoid most of the troubles and got around this course in a pleasant way despite the soaking in the first hour.

Many of the players in our group drove the final 18th hole and had eagle putts, but none of those were made. The hole, which seems to be a replica of the 18th at St. Andrews—although I was told that the reverse is true—was somewhat downwind. Most of the group had birdie putts; I was only 40 yards short of this green. A very pleasant memory to end what has become my favorite course of them all.

The trip was a phenomenal success. We got to play together and get to know one another on some of the most iconic golf courses on the planet. I was pleased with my level of play (except for Shell bunker at St. Andrews), and it's a memory that will last a lifetime.

27. An Unlikely Visit to the Old Course at St. Andrews

The year was 1985. I was making my first business trip to Europe, beginning in the company's European headquarters in Amsterdam. My meetings would start mid-week and then continue the following week at the company's semiconductor equipment division in Horsham, England, about 60 miles north of London in West Sussex.

The question was, what was I going to do for the weekend? As a relative newcomer to the company, I had no friends in Amsterdam or England, nor did I have any local knowledge of these areas.

Then a thought just jumped into my head: Why not fly from Amsterdam to Edinburgh, Scotland, and see if I could play The Old Course at St. Andrews? Even I knew it was kind of a crazy idea. I had never been to Europe before, let alone played golf at the cathedral of the game.

I had been playing golf seriously for only about six years, just long enough to give me the confidence to at least try to visit St. Andrews. I knew it was a long shot at best, but what did I have to lose? I could have done practically anything that weekend, but going to St. Andrews was something I could brag about to my friends back home.

Friends had told me about Edinburgh, so I figured that would be the place to stay. With no previous experience in Scotland, I had no clue where St. Andrews might be in relation to Edinburgh. There was good flight service there from Amsterdam, so the decision was made, and I reserved a room at the Caledonian hotel right down the street from Edinburgh Castle.

I flew out of Amsterdam on a Friday night on Air UK—dubbed YUK by the locals. Despite the nickname, the flight was uneventful, and I grabbed a cab from the Edinburgh airport to the Caledonian. I had no plan or concept of how I was going to get to St. Andrews. Remember, this was long before the internet.

Edinburgh has a nice feel to it, and the Caledonian was comfortable and welcoming. The lights from the Castle were visible from my room and provided a sense of comfort as I thought about my plan. But there really was no plan, and sleep came quickly.

I got up early the next morning and went to the front desk to ask the concierge how to get to St. Andrews. Could I take a cab? Naively, I thought St. Andrews must be close by. The concierge asked me if I drove a car, and I said I was an American with no experience driving on the left-hand side of the road. Furthermore, I had no idea where I was going, so driving was out of the question.

He directed me to Scottish Rail and told me that the train didn't go all the way to St. Andrews, so I needed to get off at Leuchars, about 6 miles from my destination. He also told me that I could take a cab the rest of the way to the Old Course, which is right in the middle of the town of St. Andrews.

It was a typical cold, damp, and gray Scottish day in the second week of November. I took a cab to the Scottish Rail station in Edinburgh and boarded the train that would get me close to St. Andrews. Although I was determined to do anything I could to play the Old Course, I had no idea whether it would be possible. I spent the hour-long train ride feeling a bit stressed, thinking about getting off the train, which was still a fair distance from my destination, with no clear idea of the steps needed to reach St. Andrews. The whole situation was starting to play into my insecurity and risk-averse tendencies.

The train ride was calming, though, with sporadic bouts of sunshine illuminating the landscape of farms and open space. What's the plan? I had no golf clubs, no golf shoes, no golf balls, and no golf attire. Nevertheless, I hoped I would figure it all out when I got there.

My stress level dropped when I got off the train and saw a short taxicab line at Leuchars. I got in the first available one and was off to St. Andrews.

In St. Andrews, there's a street that runs past the 18th hole of the Old Course, with the Royal and Ancient Club building on the right side as you turn onto it. The pro shop, starter's shed, and the first tee are on the left side of the street, and the street ends at the beach at the Firth of Forth.

It was about 11 a.m. when we turned onto that road, and I asked the cab driver if he would return at 5 p.m. to pick me up and take me back to the rail station for the return trip to Edinburgh. I was frankly amazed that he agreed to do this without any personal details from me.

He dropped me off at the British Telecom telephone booth right outside the 18th green. It was the traditional old fire-engine red phone booth (rotary dial, of course). I didn't know how to use a British phone and didn't even leave the cabbie any details . . . and there was no cell phone to call or text him.

The cab driver told me he would pick me up, and I just trusted him, although I had no reason to do so. What did I know about the reliability of Scottish cabbies? It would be dark by the time he returned for sure, as dusk arrives at 4 p.m. in Scotland in November.

I proceeded to the pro shop with little to no expectations but a burning desire to give it a shot. The shop was empty of customers, with only a gentle, engaging man who asked if he could help me. I had fully expected the St. Andrews pro shop to be full of people waiting to pay their green fees. I told him that I was a crazy American who had come to Scotland all the way from California, through Amsterdam, to realize a lifelong dream to play the Old Course. He looked at me and said nonchalantly that there was a group going off the first tee in about 30 minutes, and I could join them if I wished to.

I got very excited but told him I had no golf clubs, no golf shoes, no golfing attire. He told me, "No problem—we have clubs for you, and as for the rest, the golf shop is just across the way, and you can get whatever you need there." I really got excited now, as I was completely surprised it all fell into place so easily.

With overflowing enthusiasm, off I went into the Old Tom Morris Golf Shop to buy golf shoes (with spikes), shirt, sweater, rain jacket and hat, golf gloves, and a duffel bag to put it all in, then charged back into the pro shop. I paid my green fee of 15 pounds and joined the local threesome who were politely amused to be playing with an American who had never been to Scotland.

My comrades were three local Scotsmen who simply welcomed me into their afternoon at St. Andrews. They were amazed that I had come this far to play the course. None of them had ever been to London, let alone overseas. It was difficult for me to understand conversation as the pronounced Scottish accent takes some getting used to. The wind was howling, but we somehow kept warm, and the group proceeded to walk me through the paces of the course.

With my rented set of clubs, and without any warm-up, I teed it up on the first hole, which may be the widest fairway of any golf course I had ever played, then or now. The wind began to swirl, but the course was very quiet, with no spectators. I smacked the tee shot down the middle of the fairway, leaving me with an iron shot over the famous Swilcan Burn.

The clubs were persimmon woods and a set of Titleist irons. I was a little intimidated by the woods, but as long as I kept up with the group, I would persevere with them. I did admire the traditional Ping putter that came with the set.

These were the days when St. Andrews could be played anytime—before the lottery, the Ballot, and the New Hotel. The 17th (the Road Hole), considered the most difficult par 4 hole in all of golf, was flanked on the right by the rail yard, which would be shortly replaced by the New Hotel.

I found the tee shot on the 467-yard hole to be daunting, and I ended up having to bend a 3 wood from the rough around the railyard and back to the fairway. I managed to escape the Road Hole bunker and finished with a respectable bogey 5.

I had a glorious day on the course, staying out of the penal gorse on the right side of many holes and avoiding four-putting the monstrous greens. I felt as if I had accomplished something very special and rather crazy.

Unfortunately, I didn't escape Hell Bunker or some of its affiliates. On the 11th, I had to go backward to get out of that one, but I escaped the Valley of Sin on the 18th, made an easy par, and we were finished by 3:30 p.m. We retreated to the bar at the Rusacks Hotel, which adjoins the 18th hole.

One of the great experiences of playing St. Andrews is that the course is right in the middle of town, so you start to acquire a "gallery" of onlookers as you head for home from the 15th hole on in. I felt a little rush of adrenaline as a bunch of afternoon strollers were following us into the closing holes. People were milling about with their children, some of them flying kites on that gray day in November.

As the round ended, I couldn't believe I had pulled off my audacious goal. I still have a hard time remembering it all . . . my

strongest memory of the round is the friendliness and camaraderie of my fellow players.

Amazingly, the same taxi driver who brought me to the course
from the train station dutifully picked me up at 5 p.m. at the big
red British Telecom phone booth and took me back to the train
station.

I would return to play St. Andrews many times in subsequent
years, but nothing could be as special as playing for the first time
without any idea of whether it would even happen. It's an experience that could never be repeated.

The Old Course is a treasure. It's a bucket list item for any
golfer who has played the game, and I guarantee that the cost now
far exceeds the 15 pounds I paid for my magical round. If I were
making this trip today, the idea of just turning up and playing the
Old Course would be an impossibility, and the thought of even
trying would never have entered my brain.

Today, the Old Course is a money machine, with a strict process of getting on the course called the "Ballot." If you're an individual or small group visiting St. Andrews, you toss your name
into this daily lottery system and hope for the best.

The Ballot determines who is selected to play every day of the
year, except Sunday, when the course is closed. Tee times go off
every 10 minutes—as frequently as Pebble Beach—with a hefty
green fee to match. Most of the tee times are secured by golf
travel enterprises that arrange for their groups to play at multiple
courses throughout Scotland.

Seen through the lens of current times, my story of "walking
on" the Old Course sounds so improbable that maybe I should
have code-named it "Believe It or Not."

Iconic Golf Courses

Some of my golfing excursions are close to home; others take me quite far away. Here are some experiences at both geographic extremes.

28. Los Angeles Country Club

I had the opportunity to play the Los Angeles Country Club (LACC) North Course for the first time following its renovation after the 2023 U.S. Open. I thoroughly enjoyed the experience, except for the long 201-yard par 3, 9th hole, where I hooked my driver into the left bunker and managed to whack my bunker shot over the green. Hitting a shot over the green is the cardinal sin for this hole. The ball went sailing down the hill, and I had to muster a barrage of skills to make double bogey. The greens were just about perfect—but tricky. I did enjoy making birdie on the new par 3, 15th.

The experience jarred my memory of a prior experience many years ago at LACC. They have a club rule, not unique to LACC, that does not allow men to wear shorts on the premises for golf or any other activity. My company used to sponsor the annual John

Wooden basketball awards at the Los Angeles Athletic Club, which included a round of golf at a prestigious LA area club on the Friday before the Saturday night award show.

A number of activities taking place around the award show would typically occur on the weekend following the NCAA Final Four basketball championships. Five men and women finalists were selected for the Wooden Award; their coaches would attend the event, with the winner announced at the award banquet. In this particular long-ago year, golf was arranged at LACC for three foursomes. We briefed the players on the rules of the club and, on a Friday morning, headed off in vans provided by the Los Angeles Athletic Club to our mid-morning tee times.

One of our players was Frank Nunley (Fudgehammer), who played ten seasons in the NFL for the San Francisco 49ers from the mid-1960s to the mid-1970s. Frank was a middle linebacker who also played collegiately at the University of Michigan and was a member of the 1965 Rose Bowl-winning team. He was inducted into the University of Michigan Athletic Hall of Fame in 1989. As a football player, Frank was a mean, wild man who never seemed to be out of a play—he was always hitting somebody. He was one of the best middle linebackers in the game and played during an era of outstanding linebackers such as Dick Butkus, Ray Nitschke, and Jack Lambert.

As aggressive as he was on the field, Frank was a gentle giant and a classic gentleman off the field. I had told him about the LACC rule regarding shorts, but he didn't remember and showed up in . . . yes, shorts. Unfortunately, Frank wasn't in my van, so I couldn't remind him, and now we were at the club, a long way from our hotel. Frank always wore shorts when he played golf as a member of the San Jose Country Club. He would play in shorts even if the temperature was in the low 40s. We would always be incredulous when he showed up for an early tee time on a very cold morning, bare-legged.

We went into the clubhouse and were informed that the shorts were a non-negotiable situation. Frank was 6′2″ and 250 pounds at that time. The clubhouse manager looked at him and shook his head but said he would see if he could find some pants that might fit Frank. It wasn't looking very good, and Frank sheepishly said, "Can somebody give me a ride back to the hotel?" He looked like a guy who had lost his last friend.

The clubhouse manager eventually returned with a pair of pants that, at best, covered Frank's shins, and off we went to the driving range to warm up. Frank looked like he was wearing women's "pedal pushers," but it got the job done. Frank's golfing skills were not the greatest—although I believe he hit the best second shot I've ever seen after a "worm burner" tee shot. His golf course demeanor and behavior were first-rate, and he was always a pleasure to play with. He would apologize for hitting a bad shot and always played with speed no matter how many shots he needed.

As we completed our round, we ran into Sylvester Stallone, who was wearing pink trousers. I had trouble reconciling the rule on "shorts" at the sight of those pink pants, and I couldn't help but think that there was something wrong with this picture.

LACC was quite a treat, and the rounds there were always enjoyable. We tried to sneak a peek at the Playboy Mansion, which was located far to the right of the 14th hole. No one could have a golf-related reason to hit a ball there, but I'm willing to bet that quite a collection of severely sliced tee shots ended up there anyway.

29. The Green and the Brown in Washington State Golf

I experienced two contrasting golf venues in Washington state in a single week. The "green" is Sahalee Country Club outside of Seattle, a course as emerald as Ireland and shaped by its majestic trees. The "brown" is Chambers Bay in Tacoma, a links course with one tree, running fairways along the shore of Puget Sound, and flanked by an active rail line.

Sahalee Country Club

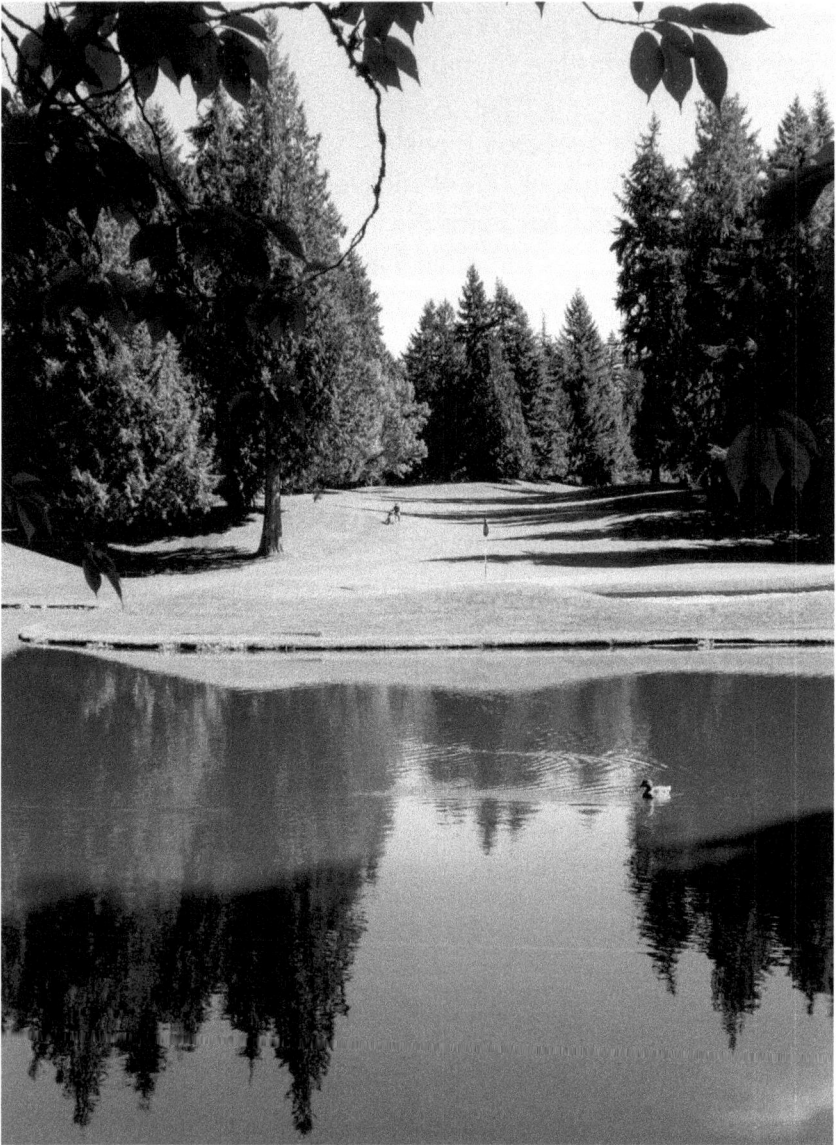

I had wanted to play Sahalee Country Club for a long time. As I pursued playing the best courses in the United States, it was one of the elusive venues to get on. I finally got the opportunity through a good friend and business associate and wasn't disappointed.

I've played a lot of golf all over the country, and I would characterize Sahalee as a religious experience, where you can compensate for your Sunday non-churchgoing by thinking about the Lord and the heavens while meandering through the beauty of this place. The course is immaculately green, with a self-proclaimed moniker of "high heavenly ground." The ground might be "heavenly," but the course may have the narrowest set of fairways I've encountered.

The course is essentially carved out of a verdant forest of cedar and Douglas fir trees that stand as gigantic green skyscrapers, shaping the view on virtually every hole. These are the largest trees I have ever seen on a golf course. References to churches continue to come to mind with the approach to every hole, as if you were heading down the aisle to the green.

The holes are consistent but not boring. Almost every hole is mesmerizing, forcing you to focus on hitting the fairway and getting into the right position to approach the green. An added feature is that you will use almost every club in your bag for all the approach shots; blasting fairway woods all day won't work to advance the ball.

There are many courses where you have to grind through four or five consecutive tough holes in a row before you get some relief as things ease up. Spyglass Hill Golf Course in Pebble Beach has this characteristic, where you play the first four holes in virtual terror as each hole gets progressively more difficult. You could be 6 to 8 over par at that point at Spyglass if things don't go well. After the 4th hole, you get to play some routine golf before it starts up again at eight and nine.

In contrast, Sahalee doesn't present the need to grind through the course. You play every hole with the same degree of concentration and focus. You have to hit the ball in the fairway with premium accuracy. Sahalee demonstrates mysterious beneficial tendencies—like when you do whack the ball into the trees, the trees simply spit it out to a lie that's either in the fairway or good enough to stay in play. It's as if your prayers are immediately answered for the errant tee shot. Every shot that my playing partners whacked into these trees was absolved, careening into the fairway or dropping into a playable lie in the rough. I did manage to miss one fairway when my ball bit the side of a tree, but it still left me with a decent lie in the rough.

This is a golf course that has been obsoleted for the PGA by its length, as the back tees are only 7,000 yards and the pros would pulverize it. The course has not had a "major" since the 1998 PGA Championship. However, it's an excellent course for the professional senior tour and the LPGA, and the club has hosted major events for both tours over the past ten years.

I would like to see the course host a PGA event. I believe it could be set up to be very difficult by further narrowing these already narrow fairways and growing the rough to the extent that it would essentially be a stroke penalty to land there. The greens are excellent and could be sped up with some onerous pin positions to create a truly credible setup.

I played the East/South configuration and enjoyed it immensely. My favorite hole was No. 1 on East, which is an opening par 5 of 500 yards. You have to hit two accurate shots to a position where you can cross the pond and avoid the back bunker to get an easy par. Hitting the two accurate shots is the key—without finding any of those trees that hug the fairway.

Another favorite hole was the par 3, 9th hole on the South, which played 181 yards. It requires a tee shot that approaches the green from the right to the proper level. Tee shots that are short or long bring the proverbial three-putt potential into this hole. I would characterize all of the holes at Sahalee as strong, because they all demand the same play: an accurate tee shot in the right place to make those pars or birdies.

Chambers Bay

We moved to Tacoma and Puget Sound to play Chambers Bay, which is the complete opposite experience to Sahalee—except that both courses were welcoming and provided excellent customer service.

Chambers Bay, a public golf course on Puget Sound, is a links course where you will not see a single tree. It's unlike any other public golf facility I have experienced. On this course, you will see a vast stretch of brownish/greenish fairways with myriad bunkers amidst some wonderful views of the sea.

Like Sahalee, Chambers Bay offers excellent customer service and welcoming staff, which is very unlike the experience at Pebble Beach, Torrey Pines, Bethpage Black, and many other famous public venues I could name. Most of those well-known public facilities believe they are doing you a favor by taking a big wad of money from your pocket and then putting up a bunch of rules to comply with. Golfers are ordinarily very compliant, so there isn't a lot of pushback to play these venues. But the Chambers Bay staff were actually welcoming, helpful, and supportive.

Chambers Bay is part of a public recreational facility that also hosts other sports, such as soccer and lacrosse. The course is walking-only, and it is quite a trek at 8 miles. The front nine, in particular, is a real hike. Chambers Bay was the site of the 2015 U.S. Open won by Jordan Spieth. The course is a traditional links layout, well bunkered with a number of interesting holes. What you see is what you get; my advice is to hit the fairways and avoid the many bunkers.

I had a few highlights, but the best one was on the 14th when I drove the ball into the fairway left bunker and had no shot to advance the ball. I simply knocked the ball out of the bunker with a sand wedge and had 168 yards to the hole for my third shot, which I hit with a 7 wood to reach 2 feet from the hole for an improbable par.

I avoided the bunker on the 18th. It's in the middle of the fairway, positioned to snatch your approach shot. Your playing partners can then watch you disappear from sight, as it's 12 feet down into this bunker. It reminded me of the Road Hole bunker at St. Andrews, except this one is meant to catch good second shots.

Two very good golf courses, with significant contrast, made for a wonderful experience in the Pacific Northwest.

30. Friar's Head, NY

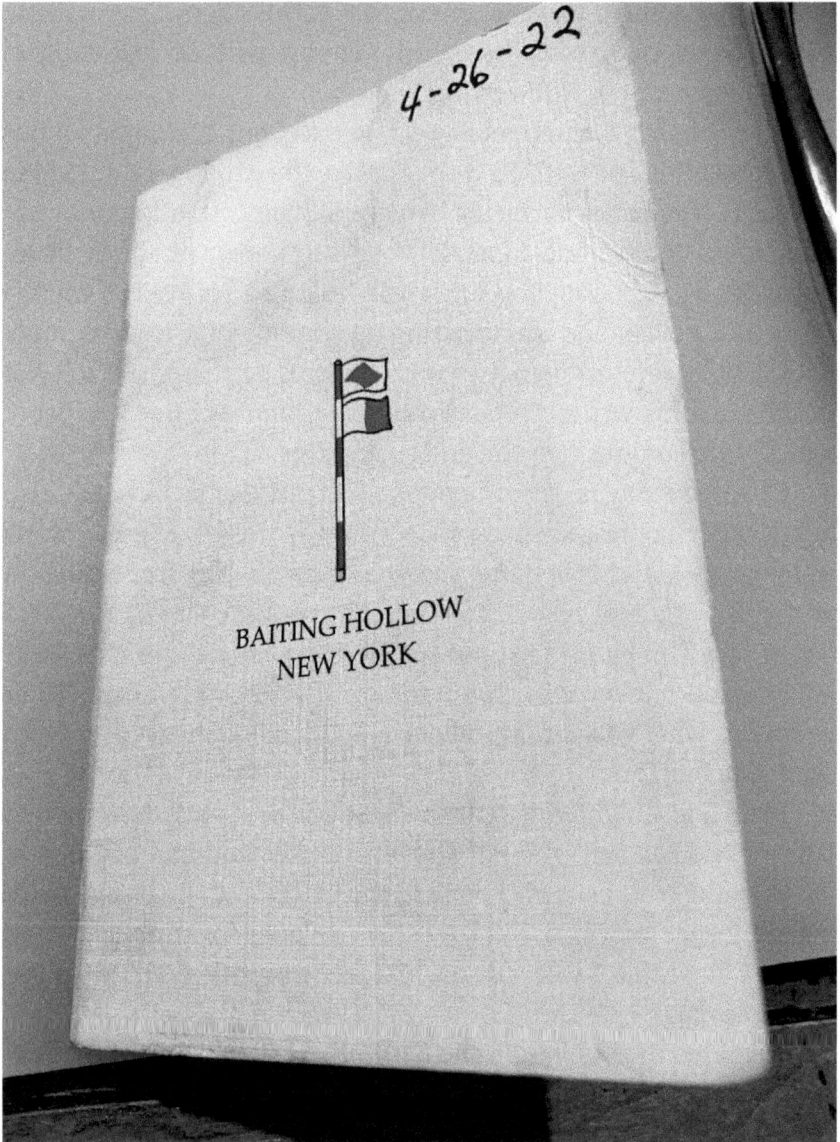

There's no sign, directions, warning, or notice of any kind that you are approaching this special place. Perhaps the entire Friar's Head venue is a gem of land that simply popped out of the Atlantic Ocean intact, ready to go.

The fairways, greens, and fescue are the equivalent of what green grass is to Augusta National. The turf is compact linksland, firm and solid as if erupting from the sea. As my playing partner and I entered the short entry drive and pressed the required buzzer to get in, it reminded me of entering Portmarnock in Dublin, Ireland—but that idea quickly faded as we encountered the empty parking lot. Out of nowhere, like a leprechaun, an affable individual emerged to say, "Playinggolf today?" We were certainly here to do that, and we would be the only players on the course this day.

I was psyched despite the 40-degree weather and 35 to 40 mph winds under bright sunny skies. It would be the first time in months that I would be walking a course, and I was wondering how my back would cooperate.

There are no golf carts at Friar's Head, so there was no option but to walk the course. My back disk issue manifests as leg pain, and I was hopeful that the adrenaline generated by being here with a caddie would enable me to really enjoy the round.

These conditions would be a true test of patience and persistence, and a good way to check if my newly retooled swing would hold up. We changed our shoes and layered up for the task ahead, replete with my 20-year-old Zero Restriction windbreaker and, most importantly, the Fairfield University beanie. My hands never get cold, but if my head gets cold, I am finished.

As we had an early rise to catch the car ferry from Bridgeport, Connecticut, to Port Jefferson, Long Island, I had to eat something. The staff at the golf course offered me anything I wanted, so I opted for a bacon and egg sandwich. It was the best one that I could remember eating. Fresh eggs and perfectly cooked bacon on an East Coast hard roll that you can never find on the West Coast.

After I scarfed down this treat, we met our caddies and headed to the range to warm up. Warming up was not warm; the wind was howling even more fiercely than at the entrance and the parking lot. I had a mindset to relax and just keep hitting good shots, sticking to tried-and-true techniques—no heroics, no pursuit of the course record, just steady play.

This would be an ethereal round. The scorecard was slightly

larger than a Post-it note, with no yardages and no hole handicaps listed. There were multiple tee boxes but only one set of tees. There were no rakes in the bunkers, as the caddies would tote rakes along with their other bag-carrying duties. There were no ball marks to repair, as the club takes care of this with their own mysterious patented technology.

The course is a wonderful walk, through dunes, fescue, farmland, and meadows. Each pin on the green has two nautical flags bearing the "F" and "H" of Friar's Head. The course got its name from sailors in Long Island Sound who believed that its sandy dunes looked like the top of a friar's noggin. There is also some similarity to the island topography of Cypress Point, with the flatness of dunes and fescue.

I struggled. The wind on the front nine was in our faces throughout. The ball was going nowhere, and my long-hitting partner couldn't achieve his usual length. I made a 45-foot putt for my first par on the par 3, 4th hole. It seemed to be pure luck and didn't instill any additional confidence. The wind was impacting my game. The gods of golf exhorted me to fix this, but it seemed a futile endeavor.

My backswing had shortened, and I knew that this was absolutely the worst thing to do. My resolve returned on the 8th hole when I told my caddie, "I am not giving up; I don't give up." I've hit too many good golf shots, and I was going to rebound. I made par on the par 3, 8th and made a decent bogey on the 9th and finished the front with a horrendous 46.

The back nine turned this round into a Dr. Jekyll and Mr. Hyde experience as we finally had some wind at our back. Par was the standard for the backside with good approach shots that enabled some one-putt pars. Because I was happy, my caddy was happy. We didn't come near a bunker or any fescue throughout the entire back nine.

The 15th hole is breathtaking. The wind was blowing so hard that we couldn't take a picture from the tee box. My partner hit a gargantuan drive that the wind grabbed and pushed far into the woods on the right. The wind almost blew the driver out of his hands when he tried to hit another ball, and that one was long gone. I found the fairway with my drive and hit what I thought was a terrific 3 wood, avoiding the left bunker about 75 yards from the green. I had to hit a 7 iron from 75 yards with the wind crossing from right to left and against (playing the distance at 150 yards). I hit this shot to 5 feet for an improbable par.

The 17th hole was about 175 yards, playing into a 30-mph crosswind right to left. The right side was a gigantic parcel of dunes and fescue, with the pin tucked into the left-hand portion of the green. The left side featured a mound of Irish-looking fescue. I'd have to aim the tee shot into the fescue, assuming the wind would grab the ball and deposit it on the green. The shot was executed well with a 4 iron into that wind, and the ball ended up 4 feet from the hole for another par.

The home hole is a wonderful par 4 of at least 400 yards, with a dogleg to the left and a fairway that will move all the shots to the right, even more so with the wind. After a decent 10-foot putt for bogey, I ended up playing the backside in 39 for a total score of 85. Three over on the backside made this round memorable for perseverance, coupled with enjoyment and great company on one of Long Island's gems.

I'm sure wind is always a factor there, but at a 10 to 15 mph clip, long hitters can go pretty low on this course. I believe putting becomes more important, especially since the greens will speed up in warmer weather. As you stroll from the 15th green to the 16th tee, you experience what makes this walk famous: the crashing waves of the Atlantic Ocean overlooking a tiny beach. It's about the eeriest feeling I have experienced on a golf course, perhaps matched only by the 11th hole at Royal Troon, where there is nothing between you and the ocean, and the quiet is deafening.

31. Golf in Massachusetts

It's the third week of October, and an explosion of brown, green, orange, and red leaves is beginning to fall from the trees. It's a quiet time of year, just ahead of the Halloween revelry. It's the time of the year when most New England golfers start to think about putting their clubs away for the winter. The more seriously committed types will continue to play and start to lose balls in the middle of the fairway under the torrent of leaves that increase in their descent from the wonderful colors we now see.

The air is crisp and clean and devoid of any pollution on this clear day as we approach Gloucester and the surrounding villages. We're headed to play in an event sponsored by *The Golf Journal*; the field will be a national contingent of members who subscribe to the publication. These events are very popular, and participants are selected by lottery months ahead of the event. Organizers customarily choose iconic venues reflecting some of the best—but often lesser-known—golf clubs in the country, many of which are private clubs with very little outside play.

Frustrated with years of losing every opportunity in the lottery, I hit the jackpot in July and was selected to play. I flew across the country from San Francisco to Boston to participate. You have to really love the game of golf to spend the money and time to get to a special venue to tee it up with a bunch of guys who feel the same way about the game as you do.

The flight to Boston was uneventful, but problems began with the rental car establishment. Despite being a premier customer with a car waiting for me to drive away, the particular car (a Jeep Wrangler, which I never rent) assigned to space B3 refused to start, after we'd already loaded our golf clubs and bags into the trunk. The upshot meant going back to the dreaded office and standing behind a line of 45 people to get to the counter to voice my problem.

After an hour in line, the rental car company promptly apologized and served up a Cadillac SUV, and we began our journey to the hotel. Thanks to the rental car fiasco, we ended up at the hotel at 9 p.m., just in time for bed in anticipation of the 7 a.m. tournament sign-in the next day at Essex Country Club.

Essex Country Club

Essex Country Club is old, but it is classic old. I felt like I was driving into a private club in the UK, though without the dreaded signage. The club opened in 1893 as a nine-hole course and eventually was redesigned by Donald Ross and became an 18th-hole layout in 1917.

The course and the clubhouse just reek of class. There's little in the way of modern amenities, but it works and is comfortable. The greens are immaculate and putt as true as they look. You can immediately surmise that this is not the course of a modern era—it's meant to be walked, as the cart paths are simply loose stones and gravel.

The course is a wonderful walk, especially in this type of coolish weather. The golf carts seemed to be vintage (perhaps circa 1980s): gas-fired chariots with clutches along with the attendant noise. The driving range was a patch of ground that could tolerate only the length of a 150-yard shot. We had a dash of England with a couple of morning showers that provided a non-disruptive spray, eventually giving way to sunshine and a gentle wind.

Essex is a course you can play every day without tiring of it. The turf of the fairways is luscious and yields wonderfully to a well-struck iron. The course presents a number of different and interesting holes. The key to scoring on this course is thinking your way around it, because the big hitter's advantage that persists in most modern courses is dissipated here. The greens are tricky but fair, with pins placed on crowns so misses can simply trail away off the green to the valley of the 3-putt.

The par 3, 4th is over 200 yards and demands a draw into a large green slightly downhill. A pond covering the entire left side of the green will receive an overcooked draw. There's no advantage to approaching the hole from the right. Two large, menacing bunkers guard the green, and any mishit to the right of those bunkers will put the ball in some horrible fescue, perhaps never to be found.

The 5th hole is a par 5 where it's important to get the tee shot in the fairway. Depending on the length of that tee shot, you'll decide whether to go for the green. But that green is guarded by a burn, which adds risk to those seeking eagle. For me, it was a 5 iron in front of the burn and a gap wedge to the green, where the pin was crowned, so the shot had to be close to secure a par.

A unique hole is the short par 4, 10th, which seems as if it might have dropped out of the sky from Ireland. The tee shot has to cover the huge mound on the right and plop in the fairway to avoid the fairway bunker. The fescue on the left creates a deterrent; a straight tee shot has only about 5 yards of fairway to get through the fescue on the left and the mound on the right. If you can navigate through this thicket, approach shots to the green will be wedges or less to make par or birdie.

Essex was fabulous. It is a course you can play every day for the rest of your existence and never be bored.

Ipswitch Country Club

Following the glorious day at Essex, we descended on Ipswitch Country Club, which I had chosen as another private club venue reasonably close to Essex. Ipswitch is as new a golf venue as Essex is old.

The club is inside a private gate of well-appointed luxury homes and resembles any number of exclusive properties. The course has every modern amenity you could think of, including a workout facility. The driving range is well-situated to the left of the club entrance and was one of the more impressive ranges I have seen in the U.S.

There is nothing Old World about Ipswitch. You won't be walking the course, as the distance between holes is significant. I suspect it might be a 7- to 8-mile trek, compared to probably 4+ miles at Essex. It's not really fair to compare the two courses. Ipswitch is a fine golf course and well-designed with a nice variety of holes shaped attractively, with receptive greens that putt well. The fairways were in wonderful condition and were almost as good as Essex.

The feel of Ipswitch is somewhat similar to Essex in its wide variety of holes and challenges throughout the course. Unlike many other New England venues, the fairways are wide enough that their trees outline the course rather than feeling like a conscious threat. There's enough width in the fairways to enable the player to focus on positions for approach shots to the green.

The first par 3 is the 5th hole of 191 yards over a pond. The tee shot has to carry the entire yardage to land on a medium-sized green, so a utility or hybrid club is probably the best choice for the average player. Any shot short or missed to the left will find the pond. The right side of the hole is protected by two bunkers, where the bunker shot will be facing the pond. I managed to avoid the bunkers on the right and scrambled a par out of an up and down.

The signature hole is the finishing hole, which is a long par 4 of over 400 yards to a severely three-tiered green. It's a tough and fair finishing hole. I had a skins game victory in my grasp as my competitors were having difficulty on the short par 4, 17th hole, but I skulled an easy 48-degree wedge shot over the green only to make bogey and lose the skin that would have clinched the match. Such is golf.

32. Amata Springs, Thailand

My playing partners and I traveled from England to Thailand to tee it up at Amata Springs Country Club in Chon Buri, about an hour north of Bangkok. We were lucky with the weather, as the usual 90-degree temperatures were down a bit due to overcast skies without any rain in sight. These conditions reduced the temperature to the low 80s, with similar humidity. We could survive the round without needing two shirts and gallons of water to stand up straight.

Amata Springs is a very exclusive club and has hosted a number of professional events, including a recent DP Tour event, Asian Tour, and women's professional events. The course was immaculate, with four sets of tees for all levels of play.

Lee Westwood holds the course record with a round of 60. Professionals can go low on this course since the fairways are well-cut and the tee shots will run, but it's hard to toughen the green speed since the prevailing humid conditions enable the players to attack the pin positions with reckless abandon.

The course is so manicured and green that you may go into a trance thinking about Augusta National. Okay, it's not Augusta, but it's very neat with little rough. Amata presents a wonderful set of visuals sculpted by a great deal of water all over the course, adding to the aesthetics rather than presenting an obstacle course.

You can score at Amata if you are long and reasonably accurate off the tee. Length is complemented by very humid conditions that are the norm in this part of the world. The greens are very receptive to spin and stop, and certainly would give the professional player birdie opportunities. You had better be accurate, because Amata has a lot of water that comes into play on many of the holes.

You should be able to avoid the water without great difficulty except for the par 3, 17th hole, which is a floating island of about 165 yards. It's similar to the infamous TPC Sawgrass hole in Florida in the Players Championship. You hit your tee shot and hope that it lands on the green. You then proceed to the launch boat, feed the koi, and make sure to have the putter in your hand. The good news about this hole is that if you land the ball on the green, it's likely to hold due to soft greens—whereas, at the TPC, you have to pray that your ball won't hit the green and head for the pond.

The surprise for our round came when we reached the 18th hole (which was our 9th hole for the day as we started on the backside). After I knocked a tee shot down the middle of the fairway, there were shrieks coming from the caddies. We had a spectator in a tree about 10 yards behind the tee: a Komodo dragon. This guy was the size of a baby crocodile, watching our tee shots.

At this point, the pace of play accelerated as the caddies scurried for the open spaces behind the tee box. They encouraged some swift movement, and our playing partners teed off quickly as we hustled through the fairway out of range of any draconian leap. We had four caddies, and their grace, beauty, and, more importantly, ability to read the greens made for a very memorable outing in Thailand.

Current State of
Professional Golf

Professional golf governance is a mess. The professional tour split between the PGA Tour (US), DP World Tour (Europe), and the LIV tour has diluted the competitive balance of the professional game to its detriment.

The PGA Tour continues to prosper as it can depend on its collegiate pipeline and the Korn Ferry Tour to help develop players. Meanwhile, LIV continues to poach and buy successful players from both tours, creating havoc and dilution for the professional game. The impact of this situation in 2024 is discussed in the following examples.

33. The 2024 PGA Tour Season (Yawn)

I must admit, I miss seeing Jon Rahm on the PGA Tour now that he's joined LIV. The 2024 PGA season got off to the usual boring start in Hawaii, with scores as low as the current state of the California snowpack. The Tour season doesn't really start for me until the professionals reach Torrey Pines in San Diego, tackling a challenging golf course.

The LIV mercenaries, changes in the broadcast booth, and the exciting finales of the NFL season have all conspired to make professional golf hard to watch. This trend continued as the nation moved into the season of March Madness, celebrating the best tournament in collegiate basketball. What made professional golf-watching even worse is that the Tour moved to Pebble Beach in what ended up as a washout, with major winter storms running right into the event.

Perhaps the gods of golf were expressing their displeasure that AT&T abandoned the venerable Pro-Am and doubled the purse to get the best players on Tour to participate. In 2023, only three out of the top 20 on Tour competed at the AT&T, and now the event is a "designated" event requiring the best players to show up and compete for a $20 million payout, up from $9 million in 2023.

Bing Crosby's legacy fun clambake event is now relegated to the wonderful memories that have accumulated over the past few years. The antics of Bill Murray throwing fans into bunkers and the on-course crooning of Larry the Cable Guy have been replaced by the prodigious drives of Rory McIlroy. I personally believe the event could use a new title sponsor that would infuse some energy, rather than sticking with an underperforming corporation that can't even provide cell phone coverage for the residents on 17-Mile Drive.

As of this writing, there is still no public resolution to the PGA Tour/DP Tour and LIV merger, which was purported to be long resolved by now. Perhaps the Saudis didn't gain admittance to the pearly gates of Augusta National, which was rumored to be a "chip" in the negotiations. Augusta National remains one of the few institutions on this planet where the value of the game of golf is more important than money. The poaching of PGA Tour players by LIV continues with the move of Tyrrell Hatton and the intense recruiting of Viktor Hovland. Hovland extinguished LIV's hopes with a two-word statement—"NO WAY"—but Jon Rahm said something similar a year ago. I believe all of these discussions are not only boring but dilute interest in professional golf.

There were some bright spots, such as Nick Dunlap's victory at the PGA West event, where the University of Alabama student and reigning U.S. Amateur champion became the first amateur to win on tour since Phil Mickelson. As for Mickelson, he seems to have disappeared into the ether of LIV's cacophony of course music and shorts, without the loyal following of his legion of fans. The PGA Champion who conquered the field and Kiawah Island is a shadow of his former favorable public persona.

The game of golf survives and thrives as play and interest at the amateur level continues to accelerate beyond the pandemic. Golf was one of the few beneficiaries of the pandemic, as millennials tired of their couch-potato existence of video games and embraced a sport that is physically and mentally challenging. A number of courses slated for closure, sale, or abandonment became cash-generating machines as the number of revenue rounds grew significantly, and it seems that the momentum has been maintained.

As for the PGA Tour, I will be surprised if TV ratings don't begin to tank except for the Major events. While professional golf management and organization seem to be in flux and rudderless, the pipeline of outstanding players at the collegiate level continues to swell, and these players will be there to populate the future of the game. It also seems that the LPGA season is off to a great start as it faces no threat of dilution from the likes of LIV, and I feel that the women's game will gain further popularity with the professional golf fan.

What about LIV? Their schedule marches on with the music, the shorts, the teams, and the inane formats that the professional golf fan doesn't recognize or understand. LIV management has no clue, or is in denial, that their events are unwatchable on TV. I've never experienced a professional sport where the spectator has no idea what is going on, and the visuals look like computer design tools.

Time will sort all of this out, but for now, it's best to go work on your handicap and enjoy the game.

34. Ryder Cup 2023

The 2023 Ryder Cup, or Circus Maximus, was played at the Marco Simone Golf and Country Club outside of Rome. I predicted a European rout over the USA that would mirror the last affair, where Team USA routed Team Europe. I used to really enjoy the Ryder Cup until it became a jingoistic carnival of drunken galleries and badly designed player attire. The current Ryder Cup gallery would qualify for attendance at a Trump rally in South Florida.

As a partisan patriotic American, I would like to have seen a different outcome, but these matches have become a 21st century version of the lions vs. the Christians in the Coliseum, with carnage everywhere. The players themselves have grown to embrace the gallery partisanship and expect boos and catcalls in the middle of their backswings.

The Cup was supposed to be a friendly competition between the countries—originally, it was the USA vs. Great Britain and Ireland, but eventually, the players from throughout Europe were added to improve the level of competition. The USA dominated the early years, but Team Europe has had its way with the Americans in the Cup's recent history.

I have a minority opinion that the behavior of the crowd impacts the level of play, which was never the intent of Samuel Ryder. The event is a huge fundraiser for the PGA of America and the Royal & Ancient, and the best players compete for bragging rights of holding onto or retaking the Cup. It's the only "all-star" team competition that has any meaning to the players, given that the all-star games in other sports such as baseball, basketball, or football are kind of a joke.

The Europeans seem to take these matches much more seriously than the U.S. You'll find considerable media coverage of the players, their intrigues, their relationships, and habits, which comes off as a version of *Entertainment Tonight*. U.S. golf fans hardly know when or where the matches are being played. The timing of the Ryder Cup in late September competes for fan attention against the almighty attraction of U.S. college and professional football.

I have to confess that I couldn't even remember who won the last Cup, but I would have guessed the USA. The last set of matches was a resounding thumping of the European squad, with the homeboy favorite, Steve Stricker, serving as Captain at Whistling Straits in Kohler, Wisconsin.

While I'm not speaking very nicely of the current state of the Ryder Cup, the players still think it's a big deal to be selected and feel very strongly about playing for their country. Selection to the Ryder Cup is automatic for half the players, but the remainder of the squad is chosen by the Team Captain, which injects some controversy into the process. There are always players who feel slighted for not being a Captain's pick.

When I looked at the 2023 team selected by Captain Zach Johnson, I had no disagreements with his choices, but one name really stood out: Justin Thomas. Normally, this selection would be a no-brainer, but Thomas had a very un-Thomas-like year and failed to qualify for the PGA Tour Championship. Thomas is a veteran Ryder Cup competitor and close to team members Jordan Spieth and Rickie Fowler, but the current state of Thomas's game would seem to bring his presence on the team into question.

The one player I believe was snubbed was Keegan Bradley, who had a terrific year on Tour, winning twice and playing very well at East Lake in the Tour Championship. I'm sure it was a close call, but Keegan was pretty disappointed, and rightly so. Thomas has been searching for his game, and the Ryder Cup is not the place to try to find it. The U.S. team was also hampered by the absence of Dustin Johnson and Bryson DeChambeau, who could not be selected for the team due to their newfound home on the LIV Tour.

Europe was well-positioned for its rout for the following reasons:

1. **Home-field advantage.** The USA has not won the Cup on foreign soil in thirty years.
2. **European golf fans take these matches far more seriously than U.S. golf fans.** The crowds were a positive factor for the Euros, as this event blasphemes all golf etiquette with cheers of "olé, olé, olé" for

every bad shot or missed putt by a USA player. There were catcalls in backswings and hoots and howls as the Americans played, while the crowd said the rosary during the European putts.

3. **Rory McIlroy was playing well.** McIlroy, the superstar of Team Europe, was the leader of the team and had some scores to settle from the last event.

4. **Team Europe was playing well.** Viktor Hovland won the PGA Tour Championship, and Jon Rahm was the player of the year with four victories on Tour, including the Masters. Tommy Fleetwood had a great year, and Tyrrell Hatton was as ferocious as ever in match play.

5. **Team Europe behaves like a team.** Meanwhile, the USA seems to be a bunch of individuals, with some exceptions; the relationships of Spieth, Thomas, and Fowler created some nucleus for the USA.

6. **The course was set up to favor the Europeans.** Long driving at Marco Simone particularly benefited Europeans.

7. **Team Europe had more momentum.** Prior to the event, Team Europe participants competed in the BMW Championship at Wentworth, which is one of the best closing events of the year on the DP World Tour. This tournament added some additional "juice" leading up to the Ryder Cup. The USA guys generally skipped the corresponding PGA event in Napa, California

The USA had its strengths, but the players who had good seasons earlier in the year weren't playing well going into the Cup matches. The media kept criticizing Scottie Scheffler's putting, which is critical in the Ryder Cup, but his tee-to-green play was still hot, and the putter is a capricious instrument that could always come around. Brooks Koepka is a keen, steely competitor who was primed to do well in Rome and break a few of Team Europe's eggs. Justin Thomas and Rickie Fowler were also ready to surprise, as they were highly motivated to make the team. Xander Schauffele and Patrick Cantlay were playing well down the stretch on tour, so they were expected to provide some fireworks for the U.S. side. On balance, though, there just didn't seem to be enough U.S. firepower to overcome the European squad.

For its part, Team Europe was also lacking some USA killers such as Sergio Garcia and Ian Poulter, whose thorns were missed due to their expulsion from the DP World Tour. Team Europe was still the overwhelming favorite.

I maintain a minority view that I would like to see these matches played in a neutral site without the screaming, hooting, and olé-ing to see exactly what these guys would do "mano a mano" without all of the BS. But that would be against the modern precept of professional golf, where money is all-important.

The Cup matches weren't even close and were over by the end of the first day. Team Europe manhandled the USA by taking a 5-point lead, which they never relinquished. Europe routed the U.S. team in one of the most savage beatings since the lions devoured the Christians in the Roman Coliseum in the first century AD. On this first day, Europe won all four matches in the opening morning sessions. At the end of day one, the matches stood at Europe 6½ to the USA 1½. These matches evoked memories of the past thirty years, as the USA has not been able to win on foreign soil since 1993 at the Belfry in the UK. Experts will propose countless reasons for why Europe beat up on the Americans this time, and all of them will be correct; the result was so resounding as to make the matches almost non-competitive.

The European side continues to be more interested in this competition. They went so far in 1979 as to add a 13th player to their squad: Seve Ballesteros. Seve was the catalyst in his day for igniting the European side to win these matches, and he provided the leadership and charisma to foster European superiority. Seve's intensity and spirit carried over to his fellow European players and provided a unifying force and focus that is rarely possible when organizing a 12-man team for competition.

In 2023, the USA needed to take the early lead to attempt to neutralize the home advantage of the crowd noise. The exact opposite occurred, as the USA was routed in the first session to the point of no return. The USA's performance the first morning spurred the home course advantage to build to a crescendo, and the American squad could provide no answers to reverse the situation.

While all the LIV players except Brooks Koepka were ineligible to play in the event, the USA squad suffered badly from the absence of some of these guys. Dustin Johnson is an experienced, successful Ryder Cupper but didn't perform well enough in the major championships to earn a spot on Team USA. Bryson DeChambeau had been playing well on the LIV Tour and would have brought some significant spirit to the USA squad. Patrick Reed, who took down Rory McIlroy at Whistling Straits in 2021, was another spark that couldn't be lit.

The Europeans also claimed some losses in Sergio Garcia, Ian Poulter, and Lee Westwood, but those guys would have added experience rather than momentum for the European side. In my opinion, the U.S. squad could have been better, but I don't believe the outcome would have been any different.

The most valuable American players in the event turned out to be Patrick Cantlay and Max Homa. World No. 1 Scottie Scheffler was shut out and played reasonably well tee to green, but the putts didn't fall, and Scheffler continues to be criticized for his putting. Cantlay provided a glimmer of hope for the USA squad with three consecutive birdies in the Saturday afternoon foursomes. Down by 2 with three holes to play, Cantlay refused to yield to McIlroy and made three consecutive birdies to win the match and win the afternoon competition 3–1. Cantlay's victory gave the USA a smidgen of a chance going into Sunday, but the Europeans extinguished that opportunity relatively quickly—particularly with McIlroy stomping Sam Burns.

The excuses kept coming, and the deafening fodder of clichés filled the airwaves, droned on by the Golf Channel and the rest of the media. Zach Johnson will not get another shot at the U.S. captaincy. It's clear he didn't understand the enormity of the challenge and what was necessary to get this team ready to play in a hostile environment. It's easy to criticize Johnson for a number of things, but the accountability buck stops at the captain. The USA still doesn't understand how to play fourball and foursomes, and the record is so one-sided that the statistics become meaningless. (How ironic that Keegan Bradley, who was snubbed from the 2023 squad, was appointed captain for the 2025 Cup.)

As an aside, to add insult to injury, I thought the Ryder Cup clothing designs for the players were the worst I've ever seen. I wouldn't be caught dead in any of this garb on the course or anywhere else.

The Ryder Cup competition has become a boring event to watch and does not portray the spirit of the game of golf that Samuel Ryder had intended. It has become the WWE/MMA version of golf at its lowest level, so rife with clichés that the only way to watch it on television is to hit the mute button.

I've had sufficient "olés" for a lifetime, and the coverage of the event provokes the most inane discussions of play that you will ever hear. There were enough "huge" putts to fill a Florida sinkhole. "The American squad" is a fabulous bunch of players with outstanding capability, "but we beat their . . ." (typical European quote). "You have to respect how good these players are but . . ." (not really). "Our team is so unified" (Europe) or "I love these guys" (USA). The tropes goes on and on. The only solace, besides hitting the mute button, might be to switch to the "Real Housewives of Augusta, Georgia."

My feeling is the only way to revive the spirit of Samuel Ryder's concept is to adopt a structure where the matches have a permanent home on each continent. I would nominate Augusta National for the U.S. site and the Old Course at St. Andrews for the European site. I would limit attendance to 10,000 spectators each day, stop the sale of alcoholic beverages completely, and neutralize all of the jingoism that this event has generated.

Of course, something like this will never happen because it would deprive the PGA of its most valuable commodity—MONEY—which is the scourge of professional golf.

35. The Open Championship

The Open Championship is the last major of the year in the post-pandemic realignment of the professional golf schedule. It's rapidly becoming the most interesting and most intriguing event and a fitting conclusion to anoint "the champion golfer of the year."

Like the 2023 winner, Brian Harman, many Open winners have been virtual unknowns in the sport. Ben Curtis (2003), Todd Hamilton (2004), and Harman were good players on the PGA Tour and, for one brilliant week, brought their A-game across the pond to capture the Claret Jug. Paul Lawrie (1999) was the eventual beneficiary of the perils of Jean Van de Velde to win at Carnoustie in a playoff. It's too painful to chronicle the mental and physical collapse of Van de Velde's 72nd hole. There have been some wonderful duels at the Open, such as the 2016 playoff between Phil Mickelson and the winner, Henrik Stenson, with both players demonstrating some incredible shot-making and putting down the stretch.

The Open is famous for the "rota," where the Royal and Ancient ("R&D") rotates play at some of the greatest links courses in the world. The players experience having to adapt to a variety of courses such as Royal Birkdale, Royal St. Georges, Royal Lytham & St. Annes, Royal Liverpool, and Royal Troon.

The Alisa Course at Turnberry was in the rota before Turnberry was purchased by Donald Trump. The British people hate Donald Trump more than stale crumpets or soggy fish and chips. The official word from the R&A was that Turnberry had lost its place in the rota because they didn't want distractions from the championship. The last Open at Turnberry was held in 2009, when Tom Watson tried to take the championship for the sixth time, only to lose it thanks to a horrible bounce on the 72nd hole. He eventually lost in a playoff to Stewart Cink. Watson demonstrated tremendous game from tee to green, defying the strength of the more powerful hitters, until his misfortune on the final hole.

Unlike the U.S. major tournaments, the Open Championship is quite an affair. Galleries at Augusta and the various U.S. Open and PGA Championship venues are limited to crowd sizes of 30,000 to 35,000 people. The Open Championship is an egalitarian affair, drawing crowds of at least 100,000 fans, who come from all parts of the United Kingdom and the world. Links courses have plenty of open space to accommodate large crowds. Galleries in the UK are knowledgeable and respectful fans, but you're going to have to grab a good spot or seat in the stands to see much of anything. The links courses allow for certain sites to get views of multiple holes of the competition.

The 2023 Open

Brian Harman brought his A+ game to Royal Liverpool for the 2023 Open. Harman was viewed, before the championship, as a PGA Tour player journeyman professional—very capable of competing with the best in the world but not among the elite. He hadn't won on the PGA Tour since 2017 but was playing very well in many recent tour events. He started to make more putts and cited changes in his putting technique. When asked to describe these changes, he treated the question as if he was being asked about some secret sauce. "I'm not going to answer that one," he stated.

He led the field in putting as well as in fairway hits. These two statistics are why Harman won the event, which would normally be the case in any tournament setting. The question was why, and why now.

The R&A did a magnificent job in setting up Royal Liverpool for the championship. It would seem that a player of Harman's caliber, who isn't among the longest drivers on the PGA Tour, would be at a disadvantage in trying to win this title.

The event requires careful focus and strategy. The longest drivers of the ball have to contend with fairway bunkers that are positioned to penalize the player by at least a half shot, if not more. Fairway accuracy is critical, as the rough produces some very unpredictable outcomes. The fescue can yield a wicked flyer or a shot that cannot attack the pin, and the greenside bunkers must be avoided completely. Based on weather conditions, the fescue could be dry or wet, generating completely different risks and results.

Harman didn't see many of those bunkers in the four days of the event, while his pursuers had enough excursions to present him with a five-shot lead going into the final round.

In 2006, Tiger Woods throttled his game back to win at Royal Liverpool on a course that was dry and fiery. Woods used his driver only twice in the entire tournament, incorporating an assortment of shots to take advantage of a course that was running hot in the July sun. Like Harman, Woods produced shots that didn't give the competitors any openings to close the gap. Woods's victory in 2006 and Harman's in 2023 happened under different course and weather conditions. Whereas Woods was able to be conservative in his approach, Harman had to be aggressive as he faced a bastion of competitors who could outdrive him considerably.

The 2023 Open Championship had a little bit of every type of weather, with some wind in the second round, reasonably benign conditions in the third round, and miserably rainy, windy conditions in the final round. The Open is unique among the major championships in that competitors so often face myriad weather issues that result in good breaks, bad breaks, and anything in between—sometimes on the same shot. Concentration, tempo, focus, and strategy all come into play.

I was impressed by Harman's waggling, which I'm sure annoyed many in the gallery. We have watched the likes of Sergio Garcia waggle to a fault in prior significant tournaments, and the question was whether this might happen again. It seemed in Garcia's case that his waggling represented indecision and a lack of confidence in what he was doing, and he was soundly criticized for it. In Harman's case, the waggling had the opposite effect, demonstrating confidence to improve the odds of execution of the shot he was about to play. For some shots, Harman waggled eight or nine times, and even more on others. The waggling seemed to reinforce what he was doing with the shot, and I found it interesting that the TV commentators made no reference to it during their broadcast.

In the final round, Harman got off to a shaky start and bogeyed the first few holes. At one point, his lead had shrunk to three shots. His response was to stay focused and not allow the bogeys to affect his concentration. His birdie on the 14th, with a masterful long putt, seemed to seal the deal.

Unlike Jean Van de Velde, who held a five-shot lead at the Open at Carnoustie, no intrusive thoughts or bad judgments permeated Harman's mind as he stepped onto the 18th tee. He didn't wimp out. He grabbed the driver, which he had mastered all week, and drove the ball into the fairway. He missed his approach shot into the greenside bunker and only had to get the ball out of that bunker and a two- or three-putt to coast to victory. Instead, he nailed the putt to finish with a well-deserved par to earn that Claret Jug.

Make no mistake, the big guns were after Harman. McIlroy played solid golf for four days, waiting for the opportunity to take advantage of Harman coming back to the field. Jon Rahm roared back from almost missing the cut to shoot a record Open score of 63 in the third round to get back into contention. Sepp Straka, Tom Kim, Jason Day, and Cameron Young were in pursuit, but Harman kept placing the ball in the fairway and never gave the field the opening they needed to close the gap.

For Young, it was the second consecutive year of being in the final group. Once again he came up short, but the gods of golf are smiling at his game. He is going to break through when it's his time.

For McIlroy, it's another top finish in a major championship without a victory, as he is not sinking enough putts in these majors to dominate and intimidate the field. But he is the best driver of the golf ball in the game today. He took on all the fairway bunkers and waved to them as his ball sailed over or around them.

Hometown favorite Tommy Fleetwood was in contention all week, but he just hit too many errant shots to get into the winner's circle. A 6 on the par 3, 17th hole on Sunday was the nail in the coffin; Fleetwood would finish 10th. He has been a stellar performer in the majors for quite a while, and you have to wonder if the gods of golf are going to sentence him to the curse of Colin Montgomerie as one of Europe's best players to have never won a major.

Harman's performance with the putter and the driver dominated the field, which is what McIlroy has to do if he is to fulfill the promise of his significant skills.

Royal Liverpool showed nicely as a tournament venue, which I had believed was a poor cousin to its neighbors Royal Birkdale and Royal Lytham & St. Annes, just up the road. The new 17th hole is a gem with its subtle Redan-like qualities, although Redan holes are usually longer (at least 170 yards); the 17th at Royal Liverpool is only 132 yards. The hole might be viewed as a younger cousin to Royal Troon's Postage Stamp No. 8 hole. No. 17 yielded a bunch of birdies and a hole-in-one, but also a bunch of bogeys and "others." The hole offers a unique challenge as a preface to the tough finishing hole.

The 18th hole played as one of the toughest challenges, demanding three excellent shots to make par. The hole is not quite as daunting as the 18th at Carnoustie, though you cannot miss either of these holes to the right.

There were a few references to the horror of Van de Velde as Harman approached the 18th hole, driver in hand. Unlike at Carnoustie, Harman waggled a few extra times and then tattooed his drive right down the middle of the fairway. The engraver of the Claret Jug could finish his work without delay.

Some Notable Professional Wins

Every once in a while, a professional wins a golf tournament in a particularly dramatic or interesting way. Here are some highlight wins from 2023.

36. Rahm Rams Through the Masters

Prior to the final round, the biggest story at the 2023 Masters was the weather. Media coverage was unending, with the pundits at CBS and the Golf Channel expending enough speculation, conjecture, and hot air to finally chase the clouds and cold weather away.

Jon Rahm played flawlessly when it mattered and pounced on third-round leader Brooks Koepka to march to victory. Rahm is the fourth Spaniard to win the Masters, joining Seve Ballesteros, Sergio Garcia, and José María Olazábal. Koepka was fabulous through the first two rounds, when he had the advantage of playing in acceptable weather compared to the rainy, windy, and cold conditions that plagued the rest of the field.

The third round was cancelled at 3:15 p.m. Eastern Daylight Time, with Koepka holding a 4-stroke advantage over Rahm and thirty holes to play. While both players were on form, it was obvious that one of these guys was on track to emerge victorious. Plenty of past Masters champions in the field know that you can always come back in this event, especially on the back nine.

By the start of the final round, Rahm had already closed the gap to 2. The omen for Sunday might have been on the very first hole, when Koepka hit the opening tee shot into the 9th fairway. He faced 215 yards to the green and had to carry a number of pine trees. Koepka's 5 iron caught the green, and he made a terrific par out of jail, but it seemed as if a struggle was about to begin.

A host of Masters Champions were rallying and posting low scores during that final round. Phil Mickelson had been playing well all week and stayed under the radar, but he kept his game together and blitzed the final four holes to finish second, becoming the oldest player to finish as a runner-up at the Masters.

Jordan Spieth made a serious run at victory, but his tee shot into the scrub brush on the 18th ended his chances, and he finished fourth.

Viktor Hovland finished seventh and had some brilliant patches, but he has yet to sustain enough consistency for 72 holes to earn a green jacket. He has the overall game to win a major, but he needs to get his short game to a higher level.

Koepka never really found it in the final round, where he shot 75 and had to settle for a second-place tie. Rahm didn't make a serious mistake on the back nine on Sunday, eliminating any hope from the field that he could be caught.

Roars from the normally silent patrons are indicators that something special is happening. One of these roars was a birdie by Mickelson as he started to make his charge on the back nine. Unlike past leaders who mismanaged their round to lose, Rahm played under control one shot at a time and kept his own pace to stay focused on victory.

Many players can be affected by what others are doing, which tends to speed up the game and cause some bad things to happen. On the dangerous, infamous par 3, 12th hole (Golden Bell), Rahm didn't go near that dangerous Sunday pin placement, choosing the left side of the green some 40 feet from the hole. Golden Bell has slain a number of past Masters leaders who either lost the event at this hole, or created so much stress that their performance and confidence were destroyed as they limped to the finish line. Rahm's back-to-back birdies on the 13th and 14th sealed the deal. On the short par 5, 15th, Rahm took no risk and decided to lay up and make an easy par en route to victory.

While Rahm was marching through Georgia on Sunday, there was the somber story of Tiger Woods. Augusta is a tough place to walk, and the cold and rainy weather made it even more difficult than expected. Tiger eked enough out of his game to make the cut for the 23rd time in a row, but he had to withdraw in the final round as his leg pain was too great to make sense for him to compete. It's hard to believe that Tiger will be able to compete further in major championships. He has all the tools and the shots, but the walking presents a severe limitation.

Fred Couples, at age 63, still has that wonderful fluid swing that enabled him to make the cut. Only one amateur, Sam Bennett, made it through the weekend. He achieved low amateur and was in contention through the first thirty-six holes, but the pressure and reality of the final round produced a few loose shots, and he tied for 16th place.

A number of great players missed the cut, including Rory McIlroy and Justin Thomas. McIlroy just couldn't get going this particular week; he didn't execute his game plan, displaying some indifferent shot-making and poor putting.

There was little to no discussion about LIV players. The Masters operates independently of the PGA Tour when it comes to the invitations. The Masters invited Koepka, Bryson DeChambeau, Mickelson, Cameron Smith, and Patrick Reed in its quest for the best field possible. LIV players played well, with Koepka, Mickelson, and Reed finishing in the Top 10. The LIV topic was completely avoided. At one point, TV viewers were treated to Larry Mize's chip shot to win the 1987 Masters on the 11th hole in a playoff. One of the participants in that playoff was Greg Norman, now head of LIV. Norman's name was not mentioned in the Mize clip.

37. Koepka Wins the PGA

Brooks Koepka, determined to overcome his failure to finish the job at Augusta, nailed the major victory at the PGA Championship at Oak Hill Country Club in Rochester, New York. Koepka was confident and completely focused on overcoming weather, elements, competitors, and distractions caused by his LIV affiliation.

Rooting against Koepka and fellow LIV players Dustin Johnson, Bryson DeChambeau, and Cameron Smith seems ludicrous to me. There's a big difference between supporting players and supporting the LIV Tour. These players are among the best in the world, and they made a choice to join a new tour for substantial compensation. At the end of the day, they are still great golfers.

During the tournament, there was the occasional booing of the LIV players, which came off as boorish behavior, reminding me of the hooligans of British football. The PGA Tour maintains its status as the preeminent showcase for professional golf. In general, golf fans will not embrace LIV due to the Saudi financing of that tour plus disdain for its combative leader, Greg Norman.

A week before the PGA Championship, Dustin Johnson and Cameron Smith were engaged in an exciting playoff in a LIV event. The television network sponsoring the LIV tour (CW—Country and Western??) cut the tournament coverage to return to regularly scheduled programming (Divorce Court?) and didn't televise the playoff. Major reporting networks such as ESPN and the Golf Channel don't cover LIV events, so no one really knows who prevailed.

LIV players may not admit it or complain publicly, but they are unhappy with their situation. They are financially satisfied and secure, but they cannot earn World Ranking points, and their public reputations have been tarnished. Golf fans have no idea how Johnson, Smith, or Koepka are performing. These players can get the opportunity to showcase their great skills at the majors only because they are past winners, eligible to participate for at least the next few years.

Smith shot 65 in the final round here and vaulted from the pack to finish ninth. DeChambeau was in contention for the entire week and finished tied for fourth place. It was a comeback week for DeChambeau, who had been recovering from injury and displayed renewed confidence in his swing. His performance added some swagger and good vibes to the tournament.

The Tournament

Koepka opened the PGA tournament with a nondescript 2 over par 72, then proceeded to play lights out from there. He grabbed the tournament lead in a rain-soaked Oak Hill in the third round. Three final rounds of 66, 66, and 67 clinched the win and enabled him to lap the field.

There were a number of subplots in the event, including multiple players in contention, combined with the adverse elements of driving rain and a difficult course setup. Jon Rahm came into the tournament riding on his No. 1 World Rank position, but this wasn't Rahm's week. He was annoyed with his play at Oak Hill, and his putting didn't respond as it had so many times before.

Rory McIlroy seemed poised to get another PGA Championship victory. He played well but could not generate enough momentum to overcome Koepka. Koepka's principal competition came from Scottie Scheffler and Viktor Hovland. For a while, it looked like Scheffler was going to persevere and take the championship, but a series of errant shots in the third round made it difficult for him to contend.

Scheffler plays with a steely determination and dispassionate inner strength that doesn't rattle under pressure. He responded from the third round with a back nine of 31 on Sunday, closing with a birdie on the difficult 18th hole to finish second.

Hovland battled Koepka hole by hole, shot for shot, but Koepka didn't yield to the pressure. On the 16th hole on Sunday, Hovland found the fairway bunker on the right side of the hole and had 140 yards to the green. He lashed at a 9 iron in the bunker, where the ball embedded at the bottom in an unplayable lie, resulting in a penalty stroke. An indifferent chip and two-putt resulted in a double bogey 6, while Koepka was calmly dropping a birdie putt. A one-shot lead became 4 shots with two holes to play. Hovland's unforced error in the bunker was the end of the tournament for him.

Koepka then pushed his tee shot on the 17th into the right rough. Unrattled, he chipped back to the fairway and proceeded to make a bogey while Scheffler was making his birdie on the 18th. Koepka's four-shot lead was down to two shots with the dangerous 18th left to play. Koepka calmly hit a terrific drive on the 18th right down the middle and nonchalantly knocked his approach shot to 15 feet for the win. Koepka's victory was a testament to his comeback from injury-riddled prior seasons, when he almost considered quitting professional golf.

The tournament also featured the spectacular play of Mike Block, a club professional from Southern California. Mike not only made the cut but also finished in 15th place at one over par and was one of only two club professionals to be within the top 20 in a major in the past twenty years. He added tremendous excitement to the crowd and a national TV audience with a hole-in-one on the 7th. He played the final round with Rory McIlroy, who was quite supportive throughout the round.

Mike became a national hero on Sunday with his finish and automatically qualified for additional events for the remainder of the season. Mike's club professional job was in abeyance for a while; students who pay him $125/hour for instruction at his club would have to wait for him. His paycheck for this event was $288,000. That adds up to a lot of lessons.

Oak Hill was a great venue. The club has hosted U.S. Opens and other USGA championships in past years and underwent some renovation in preparation for this event. It's unusual for a PGA Championship to feature rough and narrow fairways, meaning the tournament had the look and feel of a U.S. Open.

Only eleven players broke par in the tournament. Cold and rainy conditions impacted play, especially in the third round when rain teemed down all day. Oak Hill absorbed significant rain, but the greens did not take on water, and there were no puddles in the bunkers that would have suspended play. Koepka's 66 in the third round was the lowest in the field, and it enabled him to take the lead that he would not relinquish.

38. Wyndham Clark Wins U.S. Open

Wyndham Clark persevered through the late afternoon sun at the North Course of Los Angeles Country Club to claim an unlikely victory over some of the biggest names in the game, including Rory McIlroy and Scottie Scheffler. Clark's performance showed true grit with the pressure mounting on the way to the house. His birdie on the difficult 14th hole gave him a three-shot lead with four holes to play. The lead would be squandered as he fell prey to bogies on 15th and 16th.

McIlroy was pressing but failed to convert the required birdie and finished his round at 9 under par. Clark faced the final two holes with a one-shot lead but kept his focus and composure to power through. He had a 197-yard approach shot to get the ball onto the 18th green and a two-putt for victory.

His approach shot was true and safely on the green, but 60 feet away from the hole. Most of us would three-putt in a $5 Nassau from 60 feet, but Clark calmly and carefully nailed the putt to a little over a foot for the victory. The USGA allowed the crowd to surround the 18th green from the fairway, making it seem like this putt was being witnessed by the entire city of Los Angeles. The crowd noise created geometric pressure on the critical putt. Tuning out that noise to earn a major championship win exemplified the skill and focus that differentiates the professional player.

For McIlroy it was another close call in a major. McIlroy simply couldn't have played better from tee to green. His driver was spectacular, majestic, and consistent for most of the seventy-two holes. On Sunday, his performance was almost a complete replay of the 2022 Open Championship at St. Andrews.

But McIlroy didn't make a putt that mattered and would birdie only the 1st hole, which almost everybody did at some point in the competition. He needed Clark to make a mistake, and that didn't happen. In most of these majors where he is close, the competition has not faltered, leaving him to make an important putt. McIlroy is going to have to climb the last tip of the mountain, making the putts that will finally deliver a major championship win.

In prior events in 2023, McIlroy's iron play, especially short irons, wasn't good enough to convert the driving distance advantage into easier birdie putts. At LACC, his iron play improved quite a bit, so it's the putt that has to be the breakthrough component for him to convert to a major championship. McIlroy is determined to win another major, and you have to believe it will happen.

You have to feel for Rickie Fowler, who led the event through three rounds playing with Clark on Saturday and Sunday. The resurgence of Fowler's game is a feel-good story from a player who qualified for the 2022 U.S. Open as an alternate. His game hit the skids, and it has taken incredible effort and discipline to return as a star player from the abyss of his past few years of missed cuts.

The magic of the first three days abandoned Fowler on Sunday. He didn't put himself into position to attack the pins and make birdies, and his putter didn't cooperate. He was just a bit off in his distances and angles into some difficult pin placements, and the birdie opportunities were not available as he slumped to a 75 in the final round. His game continues to improve, however, and it won't be long before he enters the winner's circle again.

The dark clouds hovering over Los Angeles were a major scoring factor in the event. The USGA may have tried to exert their will to make the course as tough as possible, but Mother Nature thwarted their plan. Golf fans seem to have different expectations for the U.S. Open golf venue compared to the USGA configuration. The fans want to see "par" as the winning score and watch the professionals struggle with fairways, which the USGA has dramatically reduced in size with two levels of rough to contend with. The second cut of rough is regularly ankle deep and is at least a half- to full-shot penalty. The USGA positions penal bunkers, tough pin placements, and super-fast greens to spice up the challenge.

At this time of year, the marine layer blankets LA and much of California all the way up to at least the Napa Valley every morning with clouds, mist, and cool temperatures. The layer typically burns off by mid-morning, giving way to brilliant sunshine and a rise in temperature of at least 20 degrees. In the first round of the tournament, the marine layer hardly burned off at all, allowing the players to attack the pins with moisture from the clouds slowing down the greens.

The fairway established by the USGA for LACC North was more generous than normal, with some fairways as wide as 50 yards. As a result, records fell. Rickie Fowler and Xander Schauffele both shot U.S. Open records of 62, and there were two holes in one on the short par 3, 15th hole.

The second-round weather started in the same fashion as the first, but the marine line burned off by noon. Second-round scoring began to balloon in the afternoon. The third round saw the marine layer burn off very quickly, and the field came back to a golf course where par would be the standard. On Sunday, the marine layer persisted to just about the time when the final six leaders teed off.

Tommy Fleetwood took full advantage of the weather; he shot 63 to finish fifth. The golf course was tough for the final five twosomes, as the protective marine layer disappeared, and the course started to bare its teeth. Fleetwood might have been a factor, but he couldn't generate any birdies in his final three holes.

LACC showed well as a U.S. Open venue. The prestigious private club put on a good show. Golf fans are fickle and had some criticism of the setup, but it was a fair test for the field.

39. Corpuz Endures to Win the Women's U.S. Open at Pebble Beach

The LPGA professionals were rewarded with the opportunity to play a U.S. Open at Pebble Beach. The selection of Pebble Beach as a venue is a good indicator of the increasing popularity of the women's professional game.

Allisen Corpuz passed the exam prepared by the USGA, outlasting the field to win for the first time on the LPGA tour. Corpuz displayed significant grit and confidence while persevering through a golf course that was designed to be a difficult test. Only seven players in the field were under par. Corpuz was the only competitor with all four rounds under par, and she avoided the terrible mistakes that beset most, if not all, of her competitors.

Corpuz started the final round a shot behind Nasa Hataoka, but course conditions provided opportunities for a number of players to contend. Charley Hull was the sole player to move up the leaderboard in that round; her 66 was the best round of the day. Hull generated a mini-charge and got to within two shots of Corpuz, but Corpuz did not falter and recorded two birdies on 14th and 15th to waltz to victory.

Hull's enthusiasm was infectious and got the crowd going. She went for the 18th green for her second shot, almost pulling off this aggressive move. After her low round of 66 she finished three shots behind Corpuz. Jiyai Shin tied Hull for second with a final round of 68.

The pressure on Corpuz was enormous. In situations like these, your thoughts turn to what might go wrong as you head for the house. Corpuz had never won on the LPGA, which added pressure to achieve a first victory and a major championship. It seemed like she was in a trance. She kept her swing, repeating shot after shot by slowing things down and taking one stroke at a time.

Other competitors suffered bouts of anxiety, as a wayward drive or a missed chip shot yielded the bogies that put them out of contention. The tournament was a grind for the players from start to finish. But the experience of playing a major championship at the iconic Pebble Beach links must have been an experience they will never forget.

The USGA did a terrific job in setting up the golf course as a fair but strenuous test. The course played to 6,500 yards, and this length was a definite factor in the scoring. Holes that were played from the men's championship tees caused quite a bit of carnage for many players.

In the first round, at the 181-yard par 3, 5th hole, Lydia Ko snap-hooked her tee shot into the bushes on the left side of the hole and ended up with a 7, which was essentially the end of the tournament for her.

The 5th tee was moved forward to the regular men's tee at 142 yards, providing a breather from the continuous grind. The 8th hole, played from the men's championship tee, was "Waterloo" for a number of the players. With the wind blowing in their faces, many players had over 200-yard second shots to cross the chasm to get to the green.

Irish amateur Aine Donegan was the first-round leader. She was three under par after a birdie on the 7th in the third round, when her approach shot to the 8th green failed to cross the chasm. After going back to the drop zone, she hit another shot into the chasm, eventually recording a 9 on the hole and moving from -3 to +6. This hole would eventually cost her low amateur status as she finished one stroke behind Benedetta Moresco.

The No. 2 player in the world, Nelly Korda, hit a drive of only 154 yards on the 8th and could not navigate the chasm. Korda normally drives the ball 250 yards or more; such was the impact of the wind.

Lexi Thompson failed to make the cut, in large part due to a shot on the 8th green that did not survive the chasm. On the other side of the ledger, amateur Amari Avery hit an incredible 246-yard shot over the chasm onto the green for a routine par. Avery will be a factor on the LPGA Tour. She is a tremendous talent but has to learn the ups and downs that the gods of golf hand out from time to time.

As is usual with Pebble Beach, the scoring has to come from the first seven holes and then hang on for the remainder of the round. Birdies on the subsequent holes are few and far between. Rose Zhang, who was playing in her second LPGA championship, completed a top-10 finish. Her ball striking and all-around play was first-rate, but her putts did not go in. She had a number of makeable putts that didn't drop for her.

The USGA can be proud of what was accomplished here. At $11 million, the purse for the event was the highest that the women saw on the LPGA Tour in 2023. The women demonstrated significant skills on a golf course that was set up to be demanding, primarily due to the length of the holes and the wind. The added pressure of the USGA Women's U.S. Open made Allisen Corpuz's victory all the more satisfying.

40. McIlroy Wins the Scottish Open

The Scottish Open is traditionally the warm-up tournament for the Open Championship. It's always played the week before the Open, which is now the last major event of the year. Since 2019, the Scottish Open has been hosted by the Renaissance Club outside of Edinburgh in the town of North Berwick. In 2023, the tournament was designated as a qualifying event for the PGA Tour, with points counting toward the FedEx championship and rankings.

The course has a traditional links style, which is why the best players in the world get together to prepare for the Open Championship at Royal Liverpool. At first, scores were low and bunched up due to the absence of wind. The final round tested the players as the wind finally blew, and anything under par was considered a remarkable achievement. Such is the nature of links golf.

Rory McIlroy had been knocking on the door to win a tournament for the past several weeks, but his driving length advantage had been offset by some indifferent short irons and generally poor putting. His 2023 performance at the majors seemed ripe for a change, and perhaps the Scottish Open would be his chance.

McIlroy was in the mix with a batch of players at the top, including Tom Kim, Ben An, and Tommy Fleetwood. On Sunday, in the worst conditions of the week, Scottish professional Robert MacIntyre made a serious run at the championship, defying the windy conditions on the back nine. He started with an eagle on the 10th hole. He eventually broke through and took the lead in the tournament with a wonderful birdie on the 18th.

The par 4, 18th hole was the deciding hole. For Sunday's round, it played at a difficult 4.67. The longest drive on 18, into the teeth of a 25-mph wind, was 270 yards. MacIntyre smashed a hybrid 200 yards about 4 inches above the ground, his shot ripping through the wind and resting about 6 feet from the hole. The Scot realized that anything hit in the air would never carry the distance required.

MacIntyre holed the putt and took the lead with McIlroy still on the course, one shot behind. The toughest holes lay ahead, all facing the 25-mph wind.

MacIntyre signed his card and retreated to the Players' Lounge to await his fate. I think he would have been more confident of securing his first professional victory if anyone but McIlroy was on the course. Knowing that one of the best players in the world was still out there, MacIntyre's face seemed to combine optimism and resignation.

McIlroy battled the wind on the 17th and knocked a 6 iron to 5 feet—an unlikely birdie to tie MacIntyre. MacIntyre headed for the driving range in hopes of preparing for a playoff, as the wind on the 18th was blowing harder than ever in the late afternoon. McIlroy arrived at the 18th tee knowing he had to get this tee shot in the fairway as far as possible. He recognized that his length would be compromised by the howling wind. He backed off from hitting the tee shot three times; he had hit only three fairways all day, and he needed this one desperately.

The stubborn wind didn't die down as he launched the ball 242 yards—his usual distance for a 4 iron in normal conditions. With 202 yards to the hole, he backed off again a few times, changing clubs to a hybrid 3 club (usually a casual 5 iron) and nailed the shot to 5 feet from the hole. The putts that had eluded him over the past few events were a distant memory as he dropped the putt for the victory.

For MacIntyre, it was a bittersweet disappointment. He was deprived of a great chance at a PGA tour victory, but he didn't lose this tournament. The gods of golf decided that McIlroy had suffered enough; however, it might be that McIlroy would have traded this victory for the Open at Liverpool.

In golf, just as in life, you don't get to make those choices. MacIntyre could only smile at being beaten by one of the best players, who had to birdie the last two holes in a near cyclone to pull it off. It was clear then that MacIntyre's day would come. In fact, the gods of golf finally shed their light on him: He won the 2024 event in grand style, to the delight of the Scottish contingent that follows him.

Golf Misadventures

Emotional outbursts while playing golf are counterproductive to improving the game. As trouble mounts, the game speeds up, suppressing the good judgment and experience that players have gained through years of practice. Bad things happen at an exponential pace. In this piece, I discuss the downside of emotion, bad shots, and the ultimate insult to playing the game—the dreadful, and dreaded, shank.

41. Emotions on the Golf Course

I've always believed that golf is a microcosm of life, rather than just people chasing a little white ball around a park. Professional golfers are not immune to being buffeted by emotions while playing, but at their level, it's imperative that they learn to control them.

Most, if not all, of us have experienced anger on the golf course, even while knowing that it will only produce worse results and more horrible swings. In other sports, such as football, hockey, or even baseball, anger can raise motivational levels and lead to positive outcomes.

As a fan of the San Francisco Giants, I carry the painful memory of manager Dusty Baker giving pitcher Russ Ortiz the ball to keep as he replaced him for a reliever in game six of the 2002 World Series, as if to say, "Don't worry, it's over, we got this." The Giants were ahead 5–0 in the game and 3–2 in the series and obviously assumed they had victory in the bag. The California Angels dugout erupted in anger at Baker's act. Newly fired up, they went on to come from behind and win the game, and the World Series. Baker's act was ill-timed and disrespectful, and the Giants paid the price.

Most professional golfers will tell you that they may hit no more than three to five high-quality shots in a round of golf. To the ordinary player, this is an amazing revelation—especially when it seems that almost every shot the pros hit is perfect.

In the end, we all have the same expectation of hitting good shots. I always measure my rounds by the number of "misses" and try to keep them to a minimum. Fewer "misses" might not result in better scores, but sometimes, the overall satisfaction of playing well is more important.

Now consider the plight of one of the best players on the PGA Tour. Justin Thomas has hit an incredible number of good shots in his career, winning many tournaments and doing so with class and some pretty great play-making under pressure. He has also hit some poor shots, and I recall a number of his tee shots that meandered to the right and cost him some high finishes in major tournaments.

Nevertheless, Thomas is a force in the game and respected throughout the sport, with a string of commercial endorsements rewarding his good play and character. At the Sony Open in 2022, Thomas missed a short putt for par and was caught by a live greenside microphone using a homophobic slur after the miss. Thomas didn't even realize what he had done or understand it until he was confronted by the media at the end of the round. The resulting furor was swift and painful; companies that had sponsored Thomas or used him to endorse their products ended their association with him.

Thomas did not react with physical emotion or anger after missing the putt but uttered the slur loud enough to be caught by the microphone. He apologized publicly and learned a valuable lesson on anger and control at the highest level of the game. Thomas is not alone, but this situation was made incredibly difficult by the homophobic slur, which is disrespectful, to say the least. Because he was unaware that his words were picked up by a hot microphone, one might think that his slur is part of normal vocabulary when anger occurs on the golf course.

Emotions run high in golf (and basketball and tennis), and Thomas's got the better of him that day. You win some, you lose some. No shot is guaranteed to be executed according to one's intentions.

Tiger Woods and many other world-class players have used "f" bombs on the golf course, but this is foul language we just accept, considering most of us also do it, whether we want to admit it or not. Some people, recognizing that we are all humans and, as such, imperfect, will support Thomas's apology, and some will reject it. All he can do is shrug his shoulders and commit to doing better in the future. Endorsement deals and sponsorships are irrelevant. What's important is to recognize the failure and act on improving it.

If you recall the movie "A Christmas Story," you'll remember young Ralphie losing it when he mishandles the lug nuts while trying to help his father change a tire on the family Oldsmobile. He utters the "f" bomb for probably the first time in his life. In the 1940s, this word was not socially acceptable. Ralphie was probably just as surprised as his parents. But it did not keep them from exacting a serious rebuke on the boy, providing him with a bar of soap to munch on. I used that word only once in my household, as a 12-year-old, and sixty years later, I still regret the results of that excursion.

I will now cover the "whine," which I would define as the utterance when a golf shot doesn't meet the expectations of the player but is actually very acceptable to the rest of the players in the group. "I missed it" as the ball goes whizzing 250 yards straight down the middle of the fairway, out-driving all the other players in the group by 50 yards, is insulting to fellow players and perceived as "you guys are really terrible."

Another whine is when the player knocks the ball 50 yards out of bounds and announces to his playing partners that a shot like this hasn't happened in a round of golf in over ten years. The player feels self-vindication saying this, but the other players simply don't care and are usually unsettled by the distraction.

Father Paul Fitzgerald, President of the University of San Francisco, summarized the intent of this piece in a very elegant way: "What you are calling us to consider is this: There is a green-side microphone everywhere and always."

42. Worst Golf Shot Ever

I have seen many terrible golf shots. I once watched with complete trepidation as a player teed off on the 1st hole and almost hit a gardener who was planting flowers around the 1st tee sign at The Stanwich Club in Greenwich, Connecticut. I have seen players hit the metal tee boxes in front of them with a tremendous bang. I have seen a player in the tee box watch in horror as a player behind him hit a ball that landed 15 yards behind the tee box. I have witnessed thousands of worm burners, shanks, duck hooks, and all the rest. But none of these is as horrible as the one I am about to describe.

My wife and I live on the 13th hole of Spyglass Hill Golf Course in Pebble Beach. Our two-story home stands parallel to the 13th fairway, about 285 yards from the regular tees and 165 yards from the green. The 13th is a long par 4 that gradually moves uphill, so the fairway has little to no roll.

When the professionals play Spyglass, it's a bit unusual to see a 300-yard drive; most of the professionals and highly ranked amateurs hit drives in the 270- to 285-yard range on this hole.

It's impossible for players to retrieve some balls that trickle into the trees that make up our property. There are a number of bad golfers who have the nerve and money to play Spyglass Hill, and we are at the mercy of a poorly struck second shot.

The second shot from a terrible 150-yard drive puts our home in jeopardy. We have had three broken windows in our thirty years of owning this property. Of course, the perpetrators of these shots never admitted to them, and we had to use our own funds to make the necessary repairs.

One of the broken windows was in the dining room, which doesn't even face the golf course. I thought it would be impossible to break a window in that part of the house, as it would require a second shot that was 130 yards hooked left at a 30-degree angle. I did find a ball on my front lawn one day, which is even more difficult to execute, or even explain.

And yet, these terrible shots were not the "worst." On August 21, 2022, a new standard was created, which has a great chance of being the worst golf shot of all time.

It seemed impossible. My wife walked in from her Starbucks run and told me that there was a TaylorMade 3 right next to where she parks in front of the house. This location is about 40 yards from the dining room spot. The ball lay in our front garden about a yard from the street (Spyglass Hill Drive).

What makes the shot impossible is that it would have had to be hit left (way out of bounds) and high enough to clear the entire house. I would have loved to have seen this shot, as I just can't figure out how you could clear the house at a 30-degree angle. Perhaps the ball landed on our roof and rolled into this position, but even that would be an extraordinarily bad swing.

Spyglass Hill experiences a lot of bad shots, but this one was the worst.

43. Warning: A Visit to Shanksville, a Fabled Land of Misery

Where is Shanksville? Is it a suburb of the illusory Corona Country Club, which I've chronicled for years.

Wherever it is, it's the valley of Hades for golf. It's the resident home of the golf shot that is so awful that the word itself is almost never uttered on any golf course.

You hear plenty of swear words while playing golf, but the word "shank" will stop play completely and stun all players in the vicinity.

There is no rhyme or reason for the shank and why it appears and disappears like a wannabee Las Vegas magician. The shank cannot be produced at will. It has a complete mind of its own and strikes all levels of golfing skill without warning.

Shanksville is the way station for golfers who have been stricken with the shanks for some unknown reason by the gods of golf, or perhaps even the Almighty.

There are no defining characteristics or qualifications to become a prisoner in the land of Shanksville. Admission to Shanksville is granted as soon as the player has demonstrated the dreaded shank. The player can range from a professional to a 36 handicapper, as the shank plays no favorites.

The Grim Reaper of golf (G.R. Shank) stands guard at the gate of Shanksville. He is the St. Peter of Shanksville. Unlike Peter, however, there are no judgments or opinions determining admission. You have shanked and require immediate admittance and counseling

Shanksville is a deep, dark place of continuous moaning and groaning, with players condemned to a driving range that requires golf balls to be hit continuously until the players have purged the shanks out of their minds. They can then apply to be readmitted to their respective golf club for rehabilitation.

The Shanksville inhabitant hopes that an overnight stay is not required, as the conditions and décor at the Shanksville Marriott Hotel are rather appalling; all the rooms are painted black with no shades or curtains, and the continuous drone of "Don't Let It Get You Down" plays during the entire stay.

The guest list at the Shanksville Marriott is dotted with players from all walks of life. It's rumored that Bryson DeChambeau spent several nights there before he was able to redesign his irons and eliminate the dreaded malady. Tiger Woods made a guest appearance one week, after he &!@*#'d a five iron into the trees on Riviera's 18th hole. Tiger would later withdraw from the tournament, and one wonders about the impact of the dreaded &!@*#.

Shivas Irons, the President and CEO of the mythical Corona Country Club, has apparently spent a lot of time thinking about the scourge of the shank on the game of golf. He enlisted the services of Elon Musk, Bill Gates, and Dr. Anthony Fauci to conduct research and development into how and why the shank strikes a player in a completely random way—and how to overcome it.

Musk is building a robot (Iron Shankman) to try to replicate the potential permutations and combinations of the golf swing that produces the shank, and Pfizer is developing a vaccine that might be immediately administered to cure the shank. Fauci is doubtful that a vaccine can be developed as the disease has no symptoms other than wayward balls, but Musk believes that with AI techniques, he can successfully create the Tesla shank vaccine.

The existential challenge of dealing with the shank is that its root cause is essentially unknown; so many variables are involved in the process. Research into the topic hasn't shed light on whether the shank arises from equipment, the player, or a combination of both.

The Iron Shankman was put through a grueling set of tests with all types of equipment from Titleist, Callaway, PXG, and more. All produced almost the same horribly shanked shots during testing. Any equipment proven to be "shank-proof" would undoubtedly become the best-selling brand.

It has been represented by Donald Trump that his golf swing is "shank-proof" and that he has never encountered the shank in any shot that he has ever taken in his entire golf career. There's hard evidence from the caddies at his Bedminster Golf Club in New

Jersey that this claim is simply untrue. One caddy, who insisted on speaking anonymously, witnessed a Trump shank followed by a tantrum where the offending club ended up in the lake by the 5th hole.

Trump, without any evidence, has stated that his proprietary Trump golf ball cannot be shanked, that it can never be lost, and that it will always come to the surface of any water hazard and create a very playable lie. The Trump balls sell for $10,000 per dozen and can be found only on the Dark Web, next to the ransomware gallery.

A Trump spokesperson stated: "Trump balls represent the state of the art in golf ball technology." Therefore, the shank can be caused only by the integration of player and equipment, with the player controlling the outcome.

To this day, there is no known cure for the shank, leaving a steady stream of inhabitants entering Shanksville. As Shivas Irons sighs, "Ay, 'tis a curse of ye game."